The Astonishing Curriculum

This project was initiated by the Assembly on Science and Humanities of NCTE

Consultant Readers
ASH Officers 1991–1992

Mary Dupuis
Pennsylvania State University

Deanna Spring
Cincinnati Public Schools

Judith Gilbert
Colorado Department of Education

Beverly Sauer
University of Maine

The Astonishing Curriculum

Integrating Science and Humanities through Language

Edited by

Stephen Tchudi
University of Nevada

National Council of Teachers of English
1111 W. Kenyon Road, Urbana, Illinois 61801-1096

Staff Editor: Marlo Welshons

Cover Design: Victoria Martin Pohlmann

Interior Design: Doug Burnett

NCTE Stock Number 02107-3050

Library of Congress Cataloging-in-Publication Data

The Astonishing curriculum : integrating science and humanities
  through language / edited by Stephen Tchudi.
      p.   cm.
   Includes bibliographical references (p.   ).
   ISBN 0-8141-0210-7
   1. Language arts—Correlation with content subjects. 2. Science
and the humanities.   3. Interdisciplinary approach in education.
I. Tchudi, Stephen, 1942-   .
LB1575.8.A84   1993
428'.007—dc20   93-16053
                                                                        CIP

In Memory of

Dr. Edward Fagan
Pennsylvania State University

Founder, Assembly on Science and Humanities

Contents

Introduction

In the early 1970s, a time of progressive experimentation in the teaching of English, Ray Kytle of Central Michigan University published an unorthodox composition "book" titled *The Comp Box* (Kytle 1972). The text was not bound in conventional book covers; instead, *The Comp Box* included readings for composition packed loose-leaf, in a box. Rather than restricting readers to a prescribed sequence, Kytle invited instructors and students to order the contents for themselves.

When I met with the consultant readers of the present book to review manuscripts, we found ourselves reminiscing about *The Comp Box* and wishing we could use a similar approach. As officers of the Assembly on Science and Humanities, we wanted to prepare a book that would delve into the possibilities of interdisciplinary learning and integrated curriculum through the structuring and expressive powers of language. We found that our interrelated topics could be fenced between book covers only with difficulty. As we discussed a sequence of essays that would develop key issues in science, technology, and society, we found that we were underplaying the role of language in the creation and sharing of scientific knowledge. When we tried to order the manuscripts by language issues, we saw that our interest in crossing academic barriers failed to receive proper emphasis.

We finally discovered a way out of our predicament (short of packaging this book in a box) through the essay that now serves as the prologue. Adrian Peetoom of Scholastic Canada reminded us that in learning and language, "Little Children Lead the Way." With their "unabashedness" and their "sheer joy in moving and shaking and walking and talking," Peetoom says, young children "live life in an integrated way." And, he adds, "It will take more than a few weeks in school benches to knock this good stuff out of them." Adrian Peetoom also believes that we ought to seek curricular leadership from primary grade teachers because many of them have been at the forefront in developing integrated, whole language instruction.

The order of this bound book, then, is old-fashionedly sequential and linear: from youngest to oldest students. The Assembly on Science and Humanities offers a collection of essays that demonstrates ways of celebrating and capitalizing on the interdisciplinary and linguistic openness of young children; of enriching learning through discovery and expression in the middle, junior high, and senior high years; and of synthesizing knowledge with understanding in college and university programs of general and interdisciplinary education.

The essays are centered on classroom practice. The writers do not offer untested theoretical models or science fiction pedagogies; they describe what they have been able to accomplish in real-world teaching situations. (Interestingly enough, only two of the essays describe projects or courses dependent upon outside funding. Our writers are showing and telling what can be done within existing budgets, for the most part.) The teachers writing for this collection are also *analytic* practitioners, and in their writing the reader will find carefully articulated theories of language and learning.

A possible reading of this book, then, is cover to cover, beginning to end, letting the little children lead the way.

However, in the spirit of *The Comp Box*, I want to outline some alternative ways of reading that follow the major themes and theories of the book. There are five strong points of agreement, principles of learning, and intellectual common denominators that provide a structure for the pedagogy of integrated, interdisciplinary learning through language:

1. Bridging the Two Cultures Gap

The name of the sponsoring organization, the Assembly on Science and Humanities, is drawn from C. P. Snow's seminal essay, *The Two Cultures and the Scientific Revolution* (Snow 1959). Among our essayists, Erica Jacobs of the Jefferson High School of Science and Technology, Alexandria, Virginia, notes that when Snow identified "the rift between the sciences and humanities in 'The Two Cultures,' he could not have had today's high school students in mind." Yet the science/humanities gap clearly exists, not only in the high schools, but at all levels of education. Writing of his own high school days, Bruce Maylath of the University of Minnesota recalls a biology teacher who said, "I don't care how you write, as long as I can see that you understand biology."

The practice of isolating language from science and from other disciplines has changed some since Maylath's high school experience, and English/language arts teachers can claim a good deal of credit because of language across the curriculum programs. Yet on university campuses, in secondary schools, and even in self-contained elementary school classrooms, the predominating model of instruction not only separates the sciences from the humanities, but even isolates one science or humanities field from another: biology from chemistry, history from English, the arts from literature, vocational from academic education, and math from just about everything. The recent emergence of so-called "hyphenated" fields—psycho-linguistics, bio-chemistry, eco-feminism—provides some evidence of the felt need of some disciplines to overcome this fragmentation.

Yet, as Judith Pastore of the University of Massachusetts, Lowell, observes, "Most American education artificially compartmentalizes learning with the result that students rarely get 'the big picture'." Erica Jacobs adds that we needn't see the two cultures as doomed to isolation. We should recognize that "literary critics, writers, and historians look carefully at the world, its inhabitants, and their creations" and that "scientists do the same thing." Her point is reinforced by a teaching team of David Goodney and Carol Long, chemistry and English professors at Willamette University in Oregon. Their course, "The Literature of Natural Science," provides an outstanding model demonstrating that the contents and approaches of the sciences and the humanities are not as dissimilar as traditional schooling has implied.

Bridging the two cultures gap, then, involves seeing common intellectual and linguistic processes that are at least partly independent of the content of the disciplines. Readers who would like to explore this "two cultures" theme might alter our table of contents and examine the essays of Peetoom, Maguire and Wolfe, Jacobs, Goodney and Long, Maylath, and Pastore.

2. Demystifying Science

For most of the writers in this collection, bridging the two cultures gap requires taking some of the mystery out of science or *any* systematic field of inquiry, such as history or philosophy or mathematics or economics or literature. The fact is, we have mystified children about the learning of just about every discipline.

Our writers have chosen a series of telling metaphors to describe the way learning has perplexed many young learners. Mary Maguire and Lila Wolfe, both of McGill University, Montreal, discuss a key distinction between "cold science," with "uncritical reception of authoritative statements and questions," and "hot science," which involves "genuine reasoning and experiment." Pamela Carroll and Alejandro Gallard of Florida State University observe that in both school and college teaching, science has been treated "as either inexplicable magic or as a body of facts that can be understood simply through knowledge of key vocabulary." Dawn Abt-Perkins and Gian Pagnucci of the University of Wisconsin borrow a metaphor from Walker Percy to warn teachers against treating students as "ghosts" or semi-presences in education, mere shadows or puppets on whom the disciplines are practiced. Mike Pope of Virginia State University also uses a death metaphor to characterize much of student learning as the study of "dry bones," the dusty artifacts of disciplinary learning.

In recent years many educational reformers have called for demystifying learning in all subjects, and the writers in this book are among those who favor hands-on, inquiry-centered, holistic, discovery learning. But Karen Gallas of the Lawrence School, Brookline, Massachusetts, warns us not to be deceived by appearances of progress. She observes that although some science teaching seems inductive, "modeled to fit within the established procedures of laboratory science," often young people merely "mimic the laboratory" and thus fail to integrate or apply their learning. As Roy Fox of the University of Missouri argues, we must make further efforts to develop teaching that "immerses students in what is best about science: commitment, curiosity, discovery, focus, precision, knowledge, and facts."

To pursue a table of contents on the topic of making knowledge accessible, see the articles by Peetoom, Gallas, Maguire and Wolfe, Carroll and Gallard, Abt-Perkins and Pagnucci, Goodney and Long, Fox, Maylath, and Pope.

3. Constructing and Explaining Knowledge

The writers in this collection are concerned with much more than simple mastery of knowledge or even with taking the mystery out of learning. They want students to be knowledge makers of their own. Jane Moore and her colleagues at Baker Demonstration School, Evanston, Illinois, recognize that "children construct their own knowledge by interacting with their environment, by asking and answering questions meaningful to them, and by using and integrating materials with past and present experience in a real context." Mary Maguire and Lila Wolfe add that "schools are not only instructional sites, but cultural and sociopolitical sites as well." Thus students are constructing social as well as intellectual meanings in our classrooms.

Teachers must take knowledge out of the intellectual warehouses and see that it has "street value" for their students. Our writers agree that being academically street smart includes *metacognition*, that students not only need "to know," but also should be aware of how they go about solving problems and using language. Dawn Abt-Perkins and Gian Pagnucci show us a number of strategies they have used to assist students from "nontraditional cultural, social, and economic backgrounds" in exploring science in a summer school academy. In an essay about their work in a San Bernardino, California, middle school, Linda Prentice and Patricia Cousin explain that learning and the expression of that learning can be constructed and shared through composition in a variety of symbolic forms, including art, music, and drama.

Again there are cautionary notes: Abt-Perkins and Pagnucci warn us that constructing knowledge invariably leads to "construc*ted* knowledge" (italics added), which can, in turn, be handed down to other, passive learners. Mike Pope observes that "if meanings were gifts that could be transported through letters or sounds to learners, the teacher's task would be simply to present materials and talk." Our task is larger, he suggests, for in all fields and disciplines we are engaging students in a "composing-structuring-learning act."

Further, our essayists show that if students engage in the *process* of making meaning, they get to carry away *product* meanings. Discovery or inquiry learning does not ignore the traditional factual base of education, it simply approaches it from a different direction. If students have been involved in constructing knowledge, they are less likely to regard the edifice of knowledge as permanent or sacrosanct; they will be well prepared to replaster cracked walls, replace sagging beams, add rooms, and knock off a rococo tower or two.

To pursue the topics of constructivism and metacognition, focus your reading on the essays by Gallas; Moore, Bridgman, Shutler, and Cohn; Maguire and Wolfe; Prentice and Cousin; Abt-Perkins and Pagnucci; Fox; and Pope.

4. Integrating Study of Science, Humanities, and Society

We often hear that teachers should "make learning real" for their students. Of course, school *is* one kind of "real world," and there are compelling reasons for us *not* to pitch learners into the streets to let them construct meanings as taught by the one-room school of hard knocks. However, it is commonly acknowledged that many students perceive school and university education as being remote from issues and concerns in the world beyond the classroom. The thrust of interdisciplinary, language-based education is toward bridging that school/other-world gap, principally by showing students that "real" or "hard" knowledge, constructed by the learner, grows from experience and gives the individual a degree of control over the world.

Three essays in this collection provide examples of the process. Kathy Mathers of Washington Irving Junior High School, Colorado Springs, describes a project in which her students, offended by a newspaper article lamenting American spelling skills, launched an investigation of present-day economic and political problems. Their focused study eventually led them beyond the classroom to meet with and give their opinions to local, state, and even national political and business leaders and the media. At Colchester High School in Vermont, Betty Carvellas, Brad Blanchette, and Lauren Parren have developed an equally impressive "Science and Society" course where students of science, English, and social studies have found that they can be acknowledged as informed, literate, energized citizens. The Vermont teachers learned that connecting instruction with the real world can actually increase the rigor of academic curricula, because "confronted with real-world issues that potentially affect their lives, students invariably translate personal interest into hard work."

Equally important, real-world learning does not necessarily have to take students outside the classroom. Bruce Maylath and his colleagues at the University of Minnesota have discovered ways of making learning real to students in the biology/health program by engaging them in a publishing program where they serve as editors and writers for classroom magazines.

The notion of learning-with-consequences extends far beyond the mastery of academic disciplines. Schooling should include control over one's life as well. As Adrian Peetoom explains, "For many people, their own lives no longer seem a whole." While integrated education does not claim to lead directly to the integrated self, its ideals of interconnectedness, discovery, and application at least hint at ways in which the relationships among schools, individuals, and society might be changed.

For more discussion about connecting school and society, see the essays by Moore et al., Mathers, Carvellas et al., Maylath, Fox, and Pastore.

5. Creating a Language Base for Learning

In the twenty or so years since writing across the curriculum was first conceptualized and then practiced in the language arts, many teachers have realized that language is linked to even broader goals for school and college curricula. It's a short jump from "writing as process" to "learning as process," from "response to literature" to "response to experience," and from "whole language" to "holistic learning." Pushing the English curriculum into other disciplines has helped us perceive more fully the many roles that language plays in learning.

In her essay, Judith Pastore alludes to the work of Wittgenstein, Derrida, Foucault and others who "stress how much language molds how we perceive reality." Because science involves observing and measuring, it must list *language* among the tools of its trade. As Mary Maguire and Lila Wolfe explain: "Language and culture are intertwined phenomena. Both are very much embedded in the teaching-learning process." These writers also note that the role of language in learning is "not static, and it is not very well understood."

Three essays in this collection look directly at samples of classroom language: Maguire and Wolfe compare the flow of language in two Canadian classrooms to show how teachers' aims are reflected in their talk; Carroll and Gallard report on the teacher-student talk in a Florida science class to demonstrate conscious and unconscious use of language affecting students' understandings; and Abt-Perkins and Pagnucci discuss the language of metacognition displayed in their summer science academy.

For more on the topic of language in the curriculum, see the three essays mentioned above, or, for that matter, *any* of the essays in the collection.

One can find other possible tables of contents in this collection, and I will leave it to the reader to spot additional recurring themes, including: the role of narrative in the construction of knowledge, redefinitions of the arts and sciences, paradigm shifts in both the disciplines and teaching, the nature of a "good" question, collaborative learning and writing, creative writing and its growing links with academic prose, and the dilemma of teachers on the cusp—teachers who are exploring new pedagogical ideas in educational systems still dominated by older models. Each reader is also encouraged to discover recurring themes, issues, topics, and problems on his or her own.

Having offered alternatives for constructing our text, I will close with a rationale for reading the essays more or less in their book-bound order:

Let me ask the reader to imagine a school staffed by the teacher-writers of these fifteen essays. What a mind-boggling place it would be! The K–college curriculum would cover the following topics: trees, animals, space, castles, pyramids, astronauts, houses, dinosaurs, outer space, rocks, mammals, human differences, languages, electricity, fire, writing, wind, snow, gravity, metaphysics, dirt, pirates, decomposition, dragons, rectangles, subtraction, Africa, time, ice cream, balloons, spiders, Asia, childhood, neutrons, plain rain and acid rain, botany, bananas, the brain, animal communication, child development, Babylonia, the desert, love and hate, life and death, wonder, children's literature, adult literature, fireflies, rhetoric, global concerns, America's competitive edge, political power, parenthood, fast food, water, maps, solar systems, gender issues, literacy, nonfiction, the Frankenstein myth, exercise physiology, respiration, cardiac rehabilitation, toxic waste, euthanasia, animal rights, energy, artificial intelligence, the military, hunger, computers, television, law, astrophysics, arms control, apartheid, organ transplants, religions, biomedical ethics, addiction, consumer labeling, technological risk, atomic power, AIDS, genetic engineering, the universe and the Big Bang, and, lastly, Santa Claus, Uncle Sam, and God.

There may be gaps in this astonishing curriculum, but should they exist, I am certain that the students of these teachers could confidently and articulately fill them.

Stephen Tchudi

References

Kytle, R. 1972. *The Comp Box.* New York: Aspen Communications.

Snow, C. P. 1959. *The Two Cultures and the Scientific Revolution.* Cambridge, U.K.: Cambridge University Press.

Prologue:
Little Children Lead the Way

Adrian Peetoom
Scholastic Canada

It's a good time to be in education. The old model of schooling is being replaced by a new one, even though that may not be obvious in all classrooms. In the past, vital classroom decisions were made outside classroom doors, broad curriculum outlines handed down by some faraway administrator or curriculum committee on high, the very details of pedagogy dictated by mandated textbooks and prescribed teaching guides, and classroom time gobbled up by ubiquitous workbooks. Worse, standardized tests and lists of school-board-formulated "outcomes" often body searched each classroom for evidence of curriculum obedience.

The old model stood on a warped epistemological foundation, on notions that true knowing is a product of chopping into bits, isolating, quantifying, and abstracting. Centuries of influential thinkers kept expanding our culture's temples of numbers and facts (remember the character Gradgrind in Charles Dickens' *Hard Times*?). Their influence on schooling was enormous. Secondary education adopted its curriculum model from the university, a place increasingly misnamed the *university* as *unity* became harder to locate in institutions where specialization often made the language of one faculty incomprehensible to another. When junior high schools arose, they, too, adopted the fragmentation model, and even elementary schools at times experimented with subject-specializing teachers resident in their own classrooms to which students would travel.

Of course schools always reflect the society of which they are a part, and it would have taken uncommon wisdom and political courage to buck the culturewide trends towards individualism, spe-

---

An earlier version of this work was first published in *Prime Areas* (1990), the journal of the British Columbia Primary Teachers' Association.

cialization, and control. For instance, how did industry—also perceived as a model for schooling—justify slurping up the earth's pure water and inhaling its pure air, and after use spew them back polluted? It simply declared its technology a law unto itself, and the institution of business autonomous. "What's good for General Motors, is good for the nation," GM's Chair of the Board once said. He really meant that a factory's responsibility starts at the intake and stops at the outflow valves. It has responsibility neither to the long before nor to the much after.

The nineteenth-century traditions of education, individualism, and technology have had profound consequences. For many people, their own lives no longer seem a whole but only a collection of distinct and autonomous roles. Individual human beings have grown increasingly isolated from each other: singles within a marriage, orphans within the bosom of a family, strangers inside a friendship. Is that why clever gurus of all kinds have such an easy time gaining a following and fortune? Television preachers, politicians, self-help authors and lecturers often promise wholeness. Almost always a number of "easy" steps are required. Almost always you need to send in money.

But there are abundant signs that big changes are in the wind, some in schools. Urged on especially by vocal primary teachers, state and provincial authorities in such diverse places as Alberta, Nova Scotia, New York, Vermont, and British Columbia are suggesting that teachers make quantum leaps in professionalism by taking hold of their own classroom destinies and by building new kinds of classrooms. "Integration" is a key component of these new currents, a busy buzzword within this urgently growing educational movement.

It will take more than a few months to pour the foundations, erect the walls, and get the roofs on these new educational structures. But the will is there—as is the research—to give the builders confidence that learners—students and teachers both—can be trusted to begin seeing the world as a whole, and not to let any part of it say to the others, "I have no need of you." As a publisher, I saw the beginnings of these currents more than twenty years ago, in the integration of the language arts. I want to articulate some small account of the learning on that topic I am still doing myself:

The whole of the power of language in human life has become clearer to me over the last decades. English teachers have taught me to *listen* in the process of teaching me to understand how speech works. As they taught me the subtleties of oral language, they helped me discover—see—previously obscured facets of reading and writing. Even though I beheld the (p)arts of language emerging and becoming more distinct, more important was the emergence of the central, integrated notion that human beings learn through language.

Speaking and writing are ways of becoming clear about and making clear what we think and feel, it is true, and both language (p)arts have their technical sides that need to be learned.

But we do not speak and write in isolation. Other people hear our voices and we hear theirs, and we realize that we are inevitably concerned about the *quality* of the relationship between people. For me, cut to its essence, this relationship must be one of love. Ultimately, all people should hear foremost in my voice my interest in them as individuals, my care for them, my commitment to their welfare. If language is not centered on love concretely extended to others, it is but hollow babble.

Primary teachers seem to do this so well: to speak their love for children-barely-toddlers-no-more, to speak their care for them, their commitment to their welfare. Why primary teachers especially?

I think it has something to do with the unabashedness, with the sheer joy in moving and shaking and walking and talking that young children seem to exhibit so naturally. Primary teachers find it hard to discipline seven-year-olds, no matter how inconvenient their behavior may have been. I have not often heard the voice of primary teachers utter ridicule, contempt, and haughty superiority. You've got to be in older grades for that, or so it seems to me.

It is all captured in the picture book *The Foundling Fox*, in which a little orphan kit whimpers and attracts the attention of a vixen, mother of her own three already. She hears the voice, attends to it, and fights a hound, a badger, and a skeptic neighbor for her new-found baby. The book is about love attending to voice, and therefore also about teaching and learning (Korschunow and Michl 1985).

A set of scholars says something similar in their own register:

> The form that thinking takes inside the head is . . . a mystery, but there is no doubt that language plays a significant part in it. One thing that is known about language is that what at one stage happens openly in speech, at a later stage happens internally as thought . . . ; so there is reason to expect that by improving the quality of interpersonal language of children, we may thereby be assisting the development of thought. The idea that speech and writing are preceded by thought, and that the language act is the product of thought and learning is only

partially true: it seems also true that talking and writing *generate* thoughts and learning. (Torbe and Medway 1986, 39)

That and more I have learned about talk, real talk, talk I speak and talk I hear and talk learners produce in classrooms. When talk is a way of loving, it becomes a prime way of learning.

And so I have also learned about listening, the counterpart of talk. The vixen in *The Foundling Fox* knew how to listen! The kit's every whimper told her a story and expressed a need. Listening cannot be learned through mechanical mastery of distinct and minute listening skills. We learn how to listen by becoming intent on bonding to speakers in our life, through loving, respecting, regarding, caring. Real listening is not what most politicians do, for instance, because they only listen for those words that betray our Achilles' heels, so that issues may be advanced to help them gain power. That is why the "listening" of politicians is done by nameless and faceless public opinion poll clerks in telephone cubicles, far behind grey windows and away from the streets.

Enough has been said in the literature over the last few years about reading and writing, which has enabled all of us to quickly spin out similar observations about these elements of language. As we read books and articles, we attend to the voices-in-writing we need to hear. Writing is more than communicating with others, or struggling to come clear about the world in which we live, or storing memories in forms quickly accessible. Writing is ultimately a form of bonding with other people, a way of building loyalty, troth to an audience, whether in my case that audience is a customer, an author, a printer, or one of my grandchildren. As two Arizona primary teachers have so eloquently written, writing is first of all a way of building community (Glover and Sheppard 1989).

The traditional language arts are integrated, but not just because they come in natural pairs; for example, speakers need listeners and writers need readers. Underneath that obvious truth, they are integrated because each of them links human beings in learning about each other, and together we learn about the world through all forms of language.

And children have led the way. They did that at my home, though as a parent I often didn't see it. They have done it in classrooms, even though the official curriculum was fragmented most of the time. In schools (led by the primary grades for now), classroom strategies have begun to reflect those new insights. New classrooms are filled with children's talk and movement, with good books, toys, posters, and songs, and lots of children's writing. It is becoming rare to find beginning scholars trying to ape funny phonics sounds their teachers insist on making: *puh-uh-puh.*

Here's what language-arts integration really means, and the truth often sounds paradoxical to people still stuck in the old models. *The more we let children talk and write, the better listeners and readers they become, and the more we let them play, the better they learn.*

So much for the integration of the language arts. I also want to touch on the topic of *subject* integration, of interdisciplinary studies: language arts reaching into math, science, social studies, music, phys ed or movement, and the *vice* of language arts having many *versa*-s. It is a tricky and often misunderstood topic. I'll play with it a bit, and hold out a vision.

The picture book *A House Is a House for Me* (Hoberman and Fraser 1978) draws on the rich world of animals, plants, and people in a wide variety of shelters, living styles, and social conditions. There is a lot of geography here: rivers, seas and oceans, beaches and deserts, farmland and city backyards, jungles, and the snowy expanses where the Canadian Inuits live. To the book a reader needs to bring a knowledge of climatic conditions, raw and processed foods, clothing and play. Ordinary household goods and store-bought items appear extraordinary, and we behold their often unacknowledged contributions to our lives. Above all readers need to bring a sophisticated mastery of language to the book. (Traditional educational publishers would not want to use this book: It's too difficult for all those busy bee editors of basal readers who in their cells pretend they are once again inventing both language and teaching.)

What is more, the book works with kids of all ages, as I know from my own experiences. Why does it work? The lavish illustrations and rich text are essential components, but I think the most potent explanations for its obvious success as a source of enjoyment and learning lie elsewhere. The book touches in all of us, children and adults, a deep core of trust that somehow the cosmos in which we live hangs together in all kinds of meaningful wholes. Savour the deep satisfaction the author evokes from us when we read:

> Each creature that's known has a house of its own
> And the earth is a house for us all. (47–48)

There is not a child nor an adult who cannot understand and react to this truth with a full soul. My Christian faith reaches for any one of many passages in the Bible that speak of the wonders of creation. I have read enough world religion to know that at some stage in all faiths the splendors of the earth come to be celebrated. I have read aloud these lines some fifty times in public over the last three years, and the number of goosebumps on my body shows no sign of diminishing when I do.

> Each creature that's known has a house of its own
> And the earth is a house for us all.
>
> For the lion? Yes.
> For the cockroach? Yes!
> For the thought? Yes!
> For the bedbug? Yes!

And the earth is home to the child who in school is encouraged to discover the bewildering diversity and variety of life and objects and conditions and demands and people, and who may have some fears about getting lost and not being found again by anyone. "Am I too little?" is the question many children's books ask for them. They ask adults, "When will I ever learn?" "What will I be when I grow up?" "Who will find me when I get lost?"

We parents and teachers, lovers of children, fret plenty when we see our children fret, and we jump to reassure them. "Go ahead and try, I'll be watching." "You're so big already." "Did you do that? Marvelous!" "You'll wake up in the morning." "I'll be here when you get home." "I'll leave the light on."

But no one really spells out the whole truth to a child: The world is full of bewildered people whose institutions are fragmenting, whose relationships are cracking, who kill and maim each other for their sport, who often feel lonely in big cities and crowded in small villages. Professional football players amaze me, as coaches urge them to be animals *on* the field (Kill! Kill! Kill!), while TV interviewers elicit compassion, love of little children, and love of their mother *off* the field ("Hi, Ma!"). Fragmentation means that one can be (is often compelled to be) one person at work and another at home.

We don't always spell out these terrible truths about our modern lives for our children. It's not that our children don't sense them— they always know much more than we think—it's that we don't make the ugly truths of our lives—our failures and hopelessness—part of the curriculum, especially not for very young children. The Christian scriptures may not mean much to us anymore, but we can't help acting as if *this* text is for us all: "I tell you this: unless you turn round and become like children, you will never enter the Kingdom of Heaven"

(Matthew 19:3, NEB version). A mysterious and ambivalent text, to be sure, but one whose essence probably revolves around something, "If you can live without hope, life is not worth living." We simply know that our teaching of children must be done with hope held high. Therefore, we present the world to them in a way that makes sense, with the meaningful whole coming before the pieces.

Interdisciplinary study is inevitable if you believe that the universe hangs together in a meaningful whole. The book you are reading holds out for us that there is no theme or topic under the sun that teachers cannot treat in a rich, multidisciplinary way. We can behold its number aspects, the mass of it, the motion of it, the living of it, the feelings of and about it, the economics, the history, the language, the justice, the morality, and the faith aspects. We discover that aspects are clearly recognizable, and yet, that one aspect easily flows into another and can never be abstracted completely, set apart without links to any other aspect.

So here is my vision for the schools; it comes in two parts.

First, a classroom ought to be integrated, because life is integrated, creation is integrated. I cannot reflect on any part of life without touching upon all other parts of it. That the concept is growing in appeal only reflects that more and more people, great thinkers and ordinary people alike, have discovered what should have been so obvious. We were blinded for a while by the idols of the nineteenth-century. Abstraction and fragmentation—no matter how useful they can be in certain circumstances—constitute the rough road, not the highway to integration.

My second point is this: little children so experience life in an integrated way that it will take more than a few weeks in school benches to knock this good stuff out of them. Children have no trouble jumping from one interest to another within a theme, and often with a quicksilver logic that we adults can discover and delight in. As we look at the learning of little children to discover what learning is really like, we discover that learning is *seeing connections*. Children link the most unlikely topics and thoughts; they truly play with all there is to play with. The reason primary teachers' plans go astray more often than those of their colleagues is that their charges are too busy exploring the world the way the world presents itself to them. That is why integration never comes as a surprise to primary teachers, and that is why it is obvious that the earlier children are made to conform to fragmented curriculum and teaching approaches, the earlier they begin to dislike and to be anxious about school. We all know, don't we, that there is a qualitative difference between most kindergarteners eagerly entering school every day and most fifth graders entering resigned!

I have been an educational publisher for almost thirty years, and I have not lost my enthusiastic dreams for the potentials of learning, teaching, and schooling; nor have I lost my faith in the power of children. I have been sorely tempted to become cynical sometimes, and I have contemplated selling counterfeit promissory notes or fictitious building lots in Florida swamplands. But then I have looked at my own children and their comrades-in-play, and I have been reminded about needing to become like one of these little ones. I experienced the challenge of needing to do teaching right, a challenge also before the entire teaching profession.

I have often asked myself why people choose to work with young children. Of course there are all kinds of historical reasons: Teacher surpluses and shortages, job availability, geographic locations, and transfers of spouses all play their role. But on the whole, primary teachers seem to choose their grade levels deliberately, without being clear about their reasons. I think a major reason is the constantly pressing need to respond to children who experience the world as an integrated whole. It's not that such teachers have a lot to teach children; it's that the teachers are always being taught by the little ones. There is something in children's undifferentiated understanding that makes us feel whole and personally integrated in their presence.

This blessing granted to primary teachers becomes the challenge put to teachers of older children: namely not to be held by the siren song of fragmentation. Fragmentation and dis-integration are unnatural. They are so unnatural that it takes teaching akin to brainwashing to make children see the world as fragmented. New research is backing this notion fully; many bright scholars have seen the folly of expecting to develop better teaching and learning by simply making content more precise and distinct, objectives defined more specifically, and methodologies described more minutely. Rather, teacher-scholars observe (and learn from) children as connections-makers at home, in school, and on playgrounds. The last ten years have produced a massive body of such research, quantitative and qualitative, traditionally formatted and pathfinding, and above all readable and interesting. Many teachers like it, because it usually validates what their instincts have driven them to do for and with children. My wife likes it, because it validates what her sound parental instincts have made her do with and for our children. In fact, Johanna can get quite sarcastic about some of it, wondering why scholars become famous for describing what she did for more than twenty years with her own children at home!

This essay is a prologue, not a neat blueprint for an integrated curriculum. All I have tried to do is link the concept of integration to my lived experience in the world. But I can't help adding another potential complication, a teaser for myself as well as for the reader.

It has recently struck me that whenever we talk about children's learning, we still take for granted that there is a *core curriculum* that each child individually must master.

What if that assumption is not true? What if a classroom is a community of learners, a place where some come to know in ways others cannot? What if one child learns mostly through movement, another through reading, another through music, another through visual representation, another through logical analysis? Perhaps what matters is not the "core," but rather what the child knows specifically, or what the child doesn't know specifically, but can trust that a fellow learner *will* know and share with everyone.

So the teacher reads a book aloud, and little Carl writes a story in response. Susie doesn't always write but can dance a response. Carl can't dance, but watches Susie dance, and sees in her dance that she knows what Carl knows about the book, sort of, but she knows it differently.

Could it be that the world I seek to understand hangs together in such a way that I can only study it properly if I don't fragment one aspect from another? Is it possible that my knowing is so structurally linked to the knowing of other learners that no one is an individual knower? Are we human beings linked—integrated—together in our knowing?

These are staggering thoughts, for if there is sufficient truth in them, we must hear the death knell of the notion that competition is good for learners. Moreover, such ideas give more body to the instinct so many teachers—especially primary teachers—have about the classroom as a community of learners.

I need a lot more thinking and experience in this area before I get comfortable with it. We together need a lot more study of children as learners, knowing, as I have tried to say, that it will be children who will lead the way toward integration. I have a feeling this book will help us along mightily.

References

Glover, M., and Sheppard, L. 1989. *Not on Your Own: The Power of Learning Together.* New York: Scholastic.

Hoberman, M. A., and Fraser, B. 1978. *A House Is a House for Me.* New York: Viking Penguin Inc.

Korschunow, I., and Michl, R. 1985. *The Foundling Fox.* New York: Scholastic.

Torbe, M., and Medway, P. 1986. *The Climate for Learning.* Montclair, N.J.: Boynton/Cook Publishers, Inc.

1 Making Thinking Visible

Karen Gallas
Lawrence School, Brookline, Massachusetts

Trees have leaves. In the fall, the leaves fall off the trees. And chlorophyll goes up to the top of the whole entire tree. But when it gets colder, the chlorophyll has difficulty getting to the top of that tree, so the chlorophyll stays down for the winter, and on the next page you will find and learn more. . . .

Vera, age 6

How do children incorporate their personal understanding of the world into the knowledge they receive in schools? What began as an effort to assist children in talking and writing about science expanded to become a program on thinking about difficult questions and ideas. My focus on expanding our use of language for thinking is based on the incorporation of children's personal narratives into the study of science. It enables us to celebrate the interrelationships among the different areas of the school curriculum, and it acknowledges the holistic ways in which young children confront the process of education.

When I first implemented what we now call *science talks* and *science journals* in my first-grade classroom three years ago, I intended to assist young children in developing both their conceptualization of science, as well as their personal identity as young scientists. At the time, my theoretical rationale was based on expanding what I perceived to be the limited domain of classroom science. Generally, the teaching of elementary science is modeled to fit within the established procedures of laboratory science, and schools create structures that mimic the laboratory within classrooms. Children are taught to infer, hypothesize, identify variables, set up experimental models, carry out experiments, describe, record, and explain. We then work intensely with textbooks that are intended both to guide the teacher and to assist the child in making the world of science logical and manageable from an informational point of view. What some teachers create is a structure that makes a seemingly overwhelming field teachable, but at the same time defines or bounds the child's approach and conceptualization of science.

When studying electricity, for example, students read an excerpt from a textbook, answer questions about the text, and then conduct experiments with batteries and bulbs. In effect, the children learn to complete a circuit and light the bulb, but they often do not see the connections between the experiments and the production of electricity, because the most difficult and basic questions about how electricity is made visible in their world are rarely articulated.

Although current science teaching structures can be effective in transmitting limited bodies of knowledge about science to children, they overlook one of the key aspects of "doing" science: the relationship between scientific thinking and larger conceptualizations of the world, and indeed the universe, as an object of wonder and questioning. Often, in the early stages of studying a science unit, the students' most important and compelling questions and theories are never voiced; hence, the key concept that underlies the study itself remains obscure. For example, children's observations about lightning, blackouts, and static electricity and their risky experimentation with electrical outlets and appliances may not be called into play in the study of electricity. The many and varied observations they have made about the subject, all of which provide a rich resource for teachers, are untapped.

As a teacher of young children, I have learned that the questions children ask often reflect a very deep effort to understand their world, and that their ability to form theories about difficult questions far surpasses my expectations. Through the medium of science talks and science journals, I have seen children develop ways to make their thinking visible in narrative. In doing so, they clarified what they knew and created an expanded readiness for new information and new insights. Students also gained a stronger identity as scientific thinkers. Writing and talking about difficult ideas, building theories, asking questions—their stance as students of science changed to value their role as thinkers and knowers.

As my work continued, however, I noticed that the children I taught did not naturally confine their conceptualization of science to include only natural or physical science, and they did not communicate in ways that I associated with scientific language. Instead, they began to include narratives in their journals and their science talks that reflected broadly on the world as a whole, on the entire spectrum of life as we know it. Plants, animals, people, culture—virtually every subject became their starting point for thinking. In the process of presenting their thoughts, they used oral- and written-language devices that were sometimes more literary and poetic than expository. Metaphor, analogy, literary allusions to stories and folklore—six- and seven-year-old children were thinking and talking about their world in ways that forced me to revise my conceptualization of the purpose and potential of the science journals and science talks. As I considered the expansiveness of their views of science, I realized that when thinking about the place of wonder in children's thinking, I had assumed that children confined their amazement about the world to things scientific. Clearly they were giving me a different message: *Everything* in their world prompted a deep and reflective response.

Science journals and science talks, by eliciting children's personal narratives, enable them to discover the interrelationships between their world of experience and the many disciplines they study in school. Although it is true that these activities continue to be labeled "science activities," the children and I understand clearly that their purpose is to explore and clarify their thinking, remaining inclusive of different ways of knowing. Poetry, history, art, culture, and literature are associated and integrated with the children's constant observations of the world.

The cultivation of wonder and its validation in the child (because certainly we know that children come by it naturally) is generally not one of the stated goals of our curricula, but it is one that I believe holds great potential for teachers. By incorporating journals and talks into my curriculum, I hoped to tap into the child's internal conversations, or personal narratives, which I remember from my childhood as accompanying my exploration of the world, and which I often observed in my own children as they wandered alone outside. These conversations with oneself are filled with pondering and surprise; they contain strands of thinking and reasoning rich in association, personification, metaphor, and analogy. They also include what I call *invisible questions*, that is, unvoiced questions that children form when they encounter a phenomenon that at the time seems inexplicable: a mirage on a hot road, the rainbow of an oil spill on a city street, an encounter with a person from another culture.

In classrooms, these narratives are not normally placed in the public domain, and hence, their value as powerful tangents of thought is never tapped. Occasionally they find their way into the classroom record through informal discussions, or more subtly, as images in a painting or drawing. (If the child's thinking behind the image is solicited, however, it is clear that the tangent is part of a continuous process of developing related stories that make the world sensible and orderly [Gallas 1982].) The use of journals and talks, then, was established so children would identify this type of thinking as an important resource in school. By developing a formal structure that integrated their personal narratives into the curriculum, I hoped to prod the children into making their silent conversations public.

In discussing narrative as a literary genre, Ricoeur (1984) notes that like metaphor, narrative uses "semantic innovation" to take seemingly different and opposed experiences and synthesize them through the development of plot (ix). He characterizes this work as the result of "the productive imagination," and he notes that this process "integrates into one whole and complete story multiple and scattered events" (x). Ricoeur's conceptualization reinforces my sense as a teacher that both narrative and the metaphor that is often embedded in narrative enable children to speak about and synthesize diverse aspects of their experience, *thus making thinking visible.* If left unvoiced, this type of thinking is never crystallized, never shared, and therefore never offered for public view and comment.

Every September, I introduce the idea of the science journal to my class of twenty or so first graders. They are children of many races and ethnic groups. Many of them speak English as their first language, but often as many as a third do not. They represent all levels of the socioeconomic spectrum, and most of them cannot read. However, journal keeping has usually been a part of their kindergarten experience—a few students dictate their journals, but most are able to write using invented spelling. They understand at once that the journal is their book: a place where their most important thoughts and questions can be recorded. When I talk about keeping a science journal, there is usually a heavy silence. "What is science?" one of the children inevitably asks, and others look at him or her as if everyone knows the answer. Usually, I do not respond to that question, because I view the journal as one place where the child can begin to formulate a personal conceptualization of science. Instead I tell the children that the journal is a place to write down things we are thinking about: questions we have about our world, things we wonder about. I ask them to name a few things they have been thinking about, and we begin a list titled: *Ideas for Our Science Journals.* The children usually volunteer topics in science at first. The list includes plants, animals, space, magnets. Inevitably, one child asks if people can go on the list; soon the children are volunteering new ideas: castles, pyramids, astronauts, houses.

In the beginning of the school year, many children are tentative when approaching the journal because they are not sure what can go in one. It is as if I am the ultimate authority on what is important enough to think about. As they begin to work, I point out to them that *they* must decide what can go in the journal. Some children, believing that they are very scientific people, do not hesitate to begin writing about things they know. For them the journal starts as a place to display knowledge. They write about dinosaurs, space, rocks, mammals, and they believe that filling the pages with information is their mission. Other children are less sure. Some, in fact, can barely muster a short entry in their weekly journal time. They may draw a reluctant picture of a landscape, an animal, or a house, but they are clearly lost. Yet no matter where each child begins, the focus on the journal and the discussions with their peers and me eventually amplify every child's use of the journal and lead them to a larger understanding of what science is and how their personal stories can be an important part of their learning process.

For many children, the process of writing in their journal gives them a place to ask and possibly answer questions. Here are some of the questions they asked in September and October:

> How do scientists know all that they know? Maybe they got teached. Maybe they searched. Maybe they watched. Maybe they thought about it.

> Why do birds have feathers? Could birds fly without feathers? There are so much questions and answers that I can't keep track.

> How everything is made? It is very hard. It was very hard to make something. Like a watermelon. Something made that and something made that and on and on forever. Maybe when early humans found the things that the old people made, they figured they could make other things.

> How did the animals that were living with dinosaurs not die when the dinosaurs died?

The questions continue all year, but soon other ways of signifying stories about their world enter the journals. The children write and then illustrate their ideas, they make sketches and diagrams of something they have read or seen, or they write poems about an idea, for example:

NATURE

If winter stayed forever
trees and flowers would feel bad
because nature made them promise
that each and every year

after winter the trees would have pretty buds
and then they would turn into pretty leaves
and the flowers would have pretty buds
that would beckon.

Amy, age 6

In their journals the children, like this one, use a picture, a poem, or an observation to develop a story about something that is relevant to their study of their world of experience. For this child, the poem is a way to record her observations of the coming of spring, as well as a vehicle to express her aesthetic sense of the changing seasons and the wonder of the cycle. Her understanding of the world, which is both metaphoric and realistic, finds a place in the journal, where she expands her conceptualization of how one writes and thinks about science.

Many children move on throughout the year to use the journal as a place to think consecutively about one subject. Often the entries on a subject will continue for several weeks, as shown by the following example, which took three weeks to complete:

How come we are different?
Maybe because of our noses.
Maybe because of our babies.
Maybe because of our faces.
Maybe because of our writing.
Maybe because of our eyes.
Maybe because of our feet.
Maybe because of our lips.
Maybe because of our ears.
Maybe because of our knees.
Maybe because of our tans.
Maybe because of our tastebuds.
Maybe because of our names.
Maybe because of our moles.
Maybe because of our food.
Maybe because of our pupils.
Maybe because of our elbows.
Maybe because of our brains.
Maybe because of our smells.

Sandy, age 6

Obviously this child had been thinking long and hard about physical and cultural differences, and she had been carefully watching the people around her. Note also the form the entry takes. It is both a list and a creative composition of the child's reflections on the subject of human differences. Each line is an abbreviated representation of what was clearly a long internal narrative or thinking segment about one human difference. Some children will begin with a fascination early in the year, and will return to it periodically as they think and study more. This particular child spent much of the year writing, drawing, and thinking about people: their physiognomy, anatomy, culture, history, and foibles. Another child wrote for weeks in late winter on the subject of dirt, filling pages with a discussion of dirt, weaving into the text its relationship to animals, plants, geography, history, and himself. The following is an example of how his narrative unfolded.

> Dirt is one of the most exciting things in all of the country. In the world, there is tons of dirt. Dirt is good for flowers. Worms like it. All kinds of plants and animals like it. Pigs like it. Dirt is even good for pumpkins. Dirt is all over the sea and oceans and seashore. Clams lie around in it. Oysters like it. There is tons of it everywhere . . . Snakes like it too. They crawl on it. They just love it. Pigs lie around in it all the time like as if they were dead. There was even dirt when the dinosaurs were alive . . . Dirt is found all over the world. There is even dirt in Alaska. I love that part of the world. It has sand under the ice. . . .
>
> Andy, age 7

For this child the subject of dirt allows the mind to wander and to pull together many different ideas: things he's read in a book about pirates, experiences he's had with planting, his love for geography. His enthusiasm for the continuities in nature is expansive, and the journal provides a place where he can express that holistic attitude.

Our work in the journals continues all year, as it is an activity the children come to depend on. The journals become records of the ways in which they pull their many resources as thinkers together. At some point in the year all of the children's journals will contain drawings, sketches, and diagrams illustrating their thinking. There will be poems, stories about trips, creative writing that communicates both their factual knowledge and their aesthetic response to a topic. I place no restrictions on what form the journals should take and what belongs in them. The children have taught me to trust their ability to develop an eclectic and flexible approach in their pursuit of knowledge.

In the same way, the structure for our science talks has developed with the goal of encouraging children to discuss difficult and open-ended questions that they have generated, questions that are not

normally included in their prescribed science or social studies curriculum. In design, the talks complement the journals: Where the journal
is an individual, introverted activity that prods each child to formulate
his or her notion of what important questions and ideas might be, the
talk is directed at group or collaborative thinking and requires the
child to extrovert his or her language. Both activities leave the decision
about content in the children's hands, and both deemphasize the
centrality of the teacher's role as leader.

As with the journals, children are introduced to the talks early
in the year when they are asked to brainstorm questions they might
have about their world. I explain to them that the questions they ask
should be difficult questions they do not know the answer to, and in
fact, when a question is proposed by a child, we check to be sure that
no one does know the answer. Throughout the year the questions are
recorded on a chart, and we discuss one question each week in the
order in which they were asked. Discussions usually last from twenty
to thirty minutes. The following list includes some of the questions
that have been asked over the past few years:

> How did the universe begin?
> How do people grow?
> What makes electricity?
> How did dinosaurs die?
> How did people discover fire?
> Why are there so many different languages?
> How was nature made?
> How did writing begin?
> Does the universe end?
> How does the earth turn?
> What makes the wind?
> Are dragons real?
> Why is snow white?
> How did people change from apes into humans?

In its present form, science talk in our classroom richly represents
what happens to talk when children are encouraged to speak collaboratively and develop ideas from their own life experience. This form
developed, however, only after I had come to the painful conclusion
that my role as the moderator of science discussions was limiting,
rather than expanding, the children's thinking. Although I had assumed
that my participation in science discussions helped the children to stay
on topic, I quickly learned when I began to audiotape and transcribe
the discussions that, while they did stay on topic, it was my topic
they stayed on, rather than theirs. A comparison between a science

talk from the fall term and one later that same school year will elucidate this point as well as demonstrate what happens when the teacher's voice is kept to a minimum. The first excerpt is from a discussion of the question, "What will happen when we bury our jack-o-lantern?" It was asked by a child who wanted to bury our jack-o-lantern in dirt. ("Karen" in the text refers to me.)

> *Ollie:* Oh, Karen, Karen, I told you this before but I wanna tell the class. My friend,
>
> *Teacher:* Um hmm.
>
> *Ollie:* She has a huge, giant pumpkin outside. . .on her table, her, um, porch table, and, you see, her pumpkin has been on that table since Halloween, and it's not rotting.
>
> *Sean:* N-n-neither is one of mine rotting, and I have two . . .
>
> *Ollie:* And, and you see . . . and I think that it is because that those haven't been
>
> *Sean:* In air?
>
> *Jeff:* Outside?
>
> *Ollie:* Yeah.
>
> *Teacher:* O.K., which we talked about earlier.
>
> *Ollie:* But I've got one and you see . . .
>
> *Teacher:* O.K.
>
> *Ollie:* Remember the pumpkin that was on the step?
>
> *Teacher:* Yes.
>
> *Ollie:* It was inside but it wasn't rotting.
>
> *Sean:* But it fell down and broke.
>
> *Vera:* Well, maybe it's because you see, maybe it's because this one rotted faster, because, um, maybe it's because it was opened up, it was cut.
>
> *Teacher:* Umm. So, so what about this one that wasn't cut up and just started to rot. Remember we talked about that.
>
> *Sean:* It fell down, and blew up.
>
> *Teacher:* It didn't really . . . what do you think Chloe?

In this text, it is clear that my purpose was to help make the children's statements relate to the buried jack-o-lantern and the experiences inside the classroom. Yet the children kept making efforts to generalize to other experiences they had had with rotting pumpkins. Ollie wants to talk about her observation of her friend's pumpkin; Sean points out that only one of his is rotting. I felt that my task was to keep focusing the children, and in some cases to do that I refuted a child's remark, for example, Sean's remark that "it fell down and blew up." I mistakenly took his metaphor of falling down and blowing up to mean that Sean really thought the pumpkin had fallen. In fact, his language was describing the physical process of decomposition that one of our pumpkins had gone through. First it had collapsed, and then the whole mass had fermented and become, in effect, a larger mass of liquid and mold.

Only when I transcribed the children's remarks was I able to see that in many cases I was missing the point of their comments and limiting where they might go with their talk. By listening alone, I could not visualize the impact that my interventions were having. The process of painstakingly transcribing the tapes, and then looking carefully at what happened when I spoke, forced me to rethink the purposes and outcomes of my participation. I saw that I needed to change my level and style of participation in the talks so that the children's ideas could move to the forefront of the discussions. When I consciously withdrew my voice from the center of the discussions, the talk changed both in format and in depth, as shown by the second excerpt, focusing on the question "Were dragons real?"

> *Juan:* The dinosaurs were not, they were not dragons, but the birds they were must be dinosaurs. The dinosaur birds they were must be dragons.
>
> *Teacher:* You think they must be dragons, the dinosaurs? Juan is saying dinosaurs must be dragons.
>
> *Juan:* The birds!
>
> *Vera:* That's what I said. I said . . .
>
> *Teacher:* The birds were?
>
> *Juan:* That the birds were.
>
> *Jeff:* No they weren't.
>
> *Gary:* Cause dragons can fly, you know.
>
> *Vera:* You know, the dinosaurs might have another name, like, they might, like God might call them, uh, dragons, but we might think of them, we might call them dinosaurs.
>
> *Andy:* Or terrible lizard.
>
> *Vera:* It's just like when a baby's born and then the parents die and people don't know her real name was . . . they name her name, they give her a name.
>
> *Gary:* Um . . . um Andy gave me a brainstorm and Vera gives

> me a brainstorm. Well, Andy said dinosaur means terrible
> lizard . . .
>
> *Jeff:* Which it does.
>
> *Gary:* . . . Um . . . Vera and um, Juan said that d-, some
> dinosaurs are really dragons. Well, since dinosaurs are
> terrible lizards, dragons were terrible lizards too, weren't
> they?

As this text shows, my level of verbal participation had dropped considerably. Even when I tried to moderate the talk for Juan, who was just learning to speak English, I misunderstood his meaning, and he corrected me. What was most surprising to me as I changed my role in the talks was the way in which children worked together, as Gary says, giving each other brainstorms: collaborating, exploring, making connections among seemingly unrelated experiences, and talking in ways that I could not recognize as being scientific.

I now know that I can assist the children early in the school year by simply modeling good listening and response behaviors, rather than moderating and directing the talks. When I keep my voice out of the discussions, I find that children quickly learn to talk to one another and that the language they use is remarkable in its flexibility and its resourcefulness. As the following excerpt shows, children do not confine scientific language and thinking to a narrow expository style. They naturally use all of their narrative and poetic resources to develop theories that others can understand. This child, in trying to explain how leaves change colors in the fall, uses a metaphor of Halloween to make her point.

> I know why the leaves turn different colors. They're really that
> color . . . but you see the chlorine, whatever I mean . . . in the
> winter it stops coming up. You could even say that they're
> . . . dressing up in chlorine, and its like Halloween, that if you
> take off your coat . . . you get back to what you really are.
>
> Vera, age 7

This kind of poetic language occurs frequently in science talks, and is often accompanied by allusions to books the children have read and characters in those books that help them illustrate a difficult idea. In the following text, a seven-year-old girl tries to explain why the seasons change by speaking about the earth's position relative to the sun.

> The middle, the middle's the closest to the sun cause the sides
> aren't as close, like this is the sun (*using her hands for a model*).

> Now the sides go a little bit off . . . This is the sun, right? Now
> this is the earth. Now listen, its spinning around like this so only
> this part and this part and the like, the sun is going right for
> here, and part of the sun is, its like its breaking up and its going
> like, like Peter Pan says, he says the first shadow broke into a
> thousand pieces. Its like that, cause like the sun's breaking up.

This text is particularly striking because it shows three characteristics of science talking that six- and seven-year-olds regularly
demonstrate: using narrative or storytelling talk to develop an idea,
personifying to illustrate a point, and developing a metaphor or analogy
to make the intellectual leap toward theory. For example, this child
says the sun is "breaking up," and in alluding to Peter Pan, she
develops a poetic metaphor to illustrate the idea of how sunlight
might, in fact, break up as it hits the earth. She further develops that
thought by juxtaposing sun and shadow.

Leacock (1972) describes the power of metaphor as a tool for
abstract thinking. She notes that "through the metaphor, the relevant
characteristics of a situation are abstracted and stated in the form of
an analogy that clearly divests it of extraneous features" (129). Because
metaphor pulls an image from one context and places it in a new, and
seemingly opposed, setting, it abbreviates the connecting ideas from
the first idea to the last, and as such requires the listener to make
some leaps of thought. Generally, though, we regard metaphor as
something found in the study of poetry or literature. Yet these children
have shown that it can be used expansively to point to an idea that
is too difficult to explain in ordinary language. Talking about many
aspects of science requires the art of poetic language.

The following excerpts from a science talk titled, "What makes
the wind?" illustrate the ways children develop their ideas. What is
most important in the talks is not that the children get the right
answer. Rather, the talk provides many examples of exploratory talk,
co-construction of meaning and elaboration of thinking, as described
by Barnes (1976), and the use of personal narratives, culled from life
experience, to support the development of theory. By following the
thought process of one child throughout this discussion, and examining
the reactions of other children to those thoughts, these characteristics
can be more clearly demonstrated. Gary, who was seven years old,
quickly proposed an idea:

> You know when you're running really fast . . . I think at least a
> hundred people would run at the same time in the world.

This idea does not satisfy the group, and they struggle to understand him. In their struggle, they question, refute, and force him to reconsider his first idea. Andy objects:

> But Gary, you'll need like two thousand fifty million or more people to do, to make all that wind.

Gary rejoins:

> And there's over two thousand eight hundred and ninety-four people in the world.

Vera states her confusion:

> Gary, I really don't get it. Really, I mean . . . how could all the people, like a hundred people run in the world all together, like how . . . ?

and finally Andy clinches his logic:

> You know how there's a lot of wind in the winter. Who jogs in the winter?

By the middle of the discussion, Gary had proposed a modification of his original idea, which was generally accepted as plausible by most of the children.

> I'm sort of on the same track, only people might jog in the wind, but millions of trucks, cars might cause the wind . . . At first, the wind is just floating in the air, right, the wind is just floating around. Trucks, trucks or cars or vans or something, they come really fast, right? And when this goes this way, it cuts through all those atoms, and all those atoms go "Whup! Zoom!"

His idea was later elaborated on by the other children. One child proposed that the effects of pollution and the combination of air and gas might make wind: "like if a big puff of air and gas gets all together . . . it pushes." Throughout the discussion, other ideas are proposed and argued, as for example, the notion that rough water, caused by giant fish swimming together or fighting, makes wind. Children take observations from their own lives and attempt to relate them to the question at hand; they develop narratives to support their burgeoning theories, using their own life experience as evidence.

In building the narrative, as Ricoeur says, the process of forming a plot or a convincing story line forces the children to use critical and creative thinking strategies to synthesize what might seem to be unrelated events into a plausible explanation. In this case, Gary takes his many observations about movement: people running, cars and trucks moving fast, and with the help of other children's observations about movement, he constructs a possible narrative about what makes wind. As he does this, the other children survey their past experiences to refute or support his theory; in effect they are thinking and talking together about how this question relates to their lives.

What emerges from these talks, however, goes beyond a search for correct or right-minded ideas. Children take over the discussions and moderate their own talk; they restate preceding ideas, modify them, extend them; they question, ask for clarification, give credit for early insights and, when necessary, call for order. In fact, I have found that every child who is silent during the early talks begins to speak, question, and propose theories as the year progresses. In other words, the process of learning *how* to talk about thinking in this exploratory and collaborative manner occurs without my direct instructional intervention. The children develop ways of talking and giving voice to their thoughts that relate their personal sense of wonder about their world to their studies in school. Clearly, the development of these types of oral language skills is important for literate communication in every subject.

Thus the process of making thinking visible through oral and written narratives becomes continuous with rather than separate from the subjects we study, and it promotes an integrated view of our curriculum. Children see that their thoughts about the world should not be neatly compartmentalized into the separate disciplines of science, history, geography or literature, and that there are many ways to communicate that thinking. They realize that questions about the animal world lead naturally to considerations of human similarities and differences; that when they wonder about the beginning of languages, they must also consider the onset of writing; that a poem may best illustrate their understanding of the cycles of nature. Through the science journals and science talks, the use of personal narratives as important resources for understanding larger questions is recognized, and different ways of making sense of the world are valued. Children make tangible connections among the many subjects they study in school, and in a larger sense, relate their deep and very personal experience of the world to the process of their education.

References

Barnes, D. 1976. *From Communication to Curriculum.* New York: Penguin.

Gallas, K. 1982. Sex Differences in Children's Art. Written under surname, "McNiff, K." *The Journal of Education* 164: 271–89.

Leacock, E. 1972. "Abstract vs. Concrete Speech." In *Functions of Language in the Classroom,* edited by C. Cazden, V. John, and D. Hymes. New York: Teachers College Press.

Ricoeur, P. 1984. *Time and Narrative.* Chicago: University of Chicago Press.

2 Integrating Language Arts and Math in the Primary Curriculum

Jane Moore, Terrie Bridgman, Jean Rohner Shutler, and Ann Watson Cohn

Baker Demonstration School of National-Louis University, Evanston, Illinois

"There's a square."

Josh points to a window set in a door. A group of eighteen children and their teacher cluster around the hallway door, thoughtfully studying it. This class of first graders is engaged in a project to create a book in the style of author Tana Hoban. The activity uses the children's budding knowledge of geometric shapes to build a better understanding of the characteristics of this author.

"No," argues Kathryn, "it's a rectangle."

"What makes you think that?" the teacher asks.

"Because the sides aren't the same," she answers.

"Some of them are," the teacher points out.

Dan jumps in. "Yeah, but the two going down are longer than the other ones and squares are all the same amount long."

"Let's decide if we should put it in our Tana Hoban book," suggests the teacher.

"I think we should because it's a shape in a real place," Katie says.

But Ben points out that there is only one of them and "Tana Hoban always has lots of the things she's teaching in her pictures."

The children agree with Ben's analysis and troop off down the hallway to find more shapes. As they pass a window that looks onto the playground, Dan excitedly points to the jungle gym. "There's a whole bunch of rectangles!"

"And there are some parallelograms in it," several children announce at the same moment.

"Let's take a picture of it!"

In the primary grades, the language arts are easily integrated with science and social studies, but teachers have traditionally found it more difficult to do the same with mathematics. As faculty members of a laboratory school affiliated with National-Louis University, we have worked as a group to find natural, mutually productive connections between language arts and math. In our varied roles as primary grade teachers and teacher educators, we have been confronted with the need to discover ways to further implement and model the integrated curriculum we advocate to our college students.

During the past two years we have identified and successfully implemented four means of integrating various areas of the language arts into the mathematics curriculum. The four strands are: creating stories by transferring real-life math situations into oral, pictorial, and written accounts; using children's literature as a venue for developing math concepts; developing oral articulation through group problem solving; and developing writing skills and math concepts through the use of math journals.

As we examined current guidelines for best practice from such organizations as the National Association for the Education of Young Children (NAEYC) and the National Council of Teachers of Mathematics (NCTM), we noted some striking similarities. Specialists claim that children construct their own knowledge by interacting with their environment, by asking and answering questions meaningful to them, and by using and integrating materials with past and present experiences in a real context. The language-rich environment is a catalyst for building mathematical concepts in the early grades. Oral language is the "warp" thread in the mathematical tapestry; the language of mathematics becomes woven into the child's daily language.

Our work at Baker School built on these theories, providing a practical context in which to view them. Though presented within the framework of particular grades, all four strands are found throughout our primary program.

Terrie Bridgman, Grade 1

Students arrive in my first-grade class every year with the wonderful ability to talk about anything! They have countless stories about everything from trips to the dentist to a new puppy. Their enthusiasm appears endless when someone gives them the invitation: "Tell me about it." These discourses are generally delivered in a well-articulated and organized fashion. My conclusion is that children not only love to talk, but that they also need to be allowed to use language to make sense out of their world. As children are introduced to novel concepts, it is essential that they use oral language to internalize their understandings. It is my firm belief in the importance of oral language that drives my first-grade math program. The children in my class are presented with mathematical problems and ideas to explore with concrete manipulatives; they are also given a multitude of opportunities to talk about these situations. I present math to my class as a subject that we talk about, just as we do other topics in school. With this reverence for talking about math, my class decided this year to have a "Subtraction Fair." We planned the event so that our neighboring kindergartners could hear our own subtraction stories.

The preparation started long before the children had generated the idea for the fair. I had introduced the concept of subtraction by telling the children numerous stories that involved the process of subtraction. Unlike the stories that are found in workbooks, these stories were realistic ones that involved events that occurred in everyday life. After I was sure that the children were familiar with subtraction terminology, I gave them manipulatives to act out the stories. Traditionally the next step would be to show the children the symbols involved in subtraction algorithms and to demonstrate their use. However, it has been my experience that for many children this step is made prematurely and causes undue confusion. Instead, I have found the math program needs to provide opportunities for children to develop and articulate their own math stories. As the students formulate their own stories, they should also be given materials to demonstrate their tales. The children in my class have enjoyed this step so much that I always find myself adjusting my plans for additional story days! This year the adjustment in my plan book became the Subtraction Fair.

The first component of the fair was the writing of invitations to assigned kindergarten partners. Next, individual stories were composed and written by each student using his or her own developmental writing system. I could tell the children had been sold on the project when I heard their stories. One child wrote this wonderful story about an African hunting expedition:

> Once upon a time two hunters went on an African safari. They caught six giraffes. The hunters gave the giraffes to the Lincoln

> Park Zoo. The giraffes hated the zoo and two of them ran away.
> How many were left in the zoo?

After an editing session with the teacher, the children copied their stories onto large pieces of construction paper. These stories were taped on their desks as the first part of the fair exhibit. The children also decided that rather than use manipulatives from the classroom supply to demonstrate their stories, they would make their own. For the next two days math time was devoted to manufacturing artifacts that could be used when the stories were told. Children spent hours constructing such items as ice cream cones for stories about hungry siblings and balloons that would be blown away by the wind.

At no time during the preparation period did we talk as a class about how we were going to teach our guests about subtraction. I had made the decision to take the back seat in this production. I knew the children would be encouraged to collaborate during the preparation process on how they would entertain our guests. After a week of talking, writing, and making manipulatives, our fair was complete and ready for our neighbors.

When the kindergarten class arrived, we had an appointed spokesperson tell them the procedures for visiting our exhibits. The children first told their subtraction stories to their partners and then gave a detailed retelling of the account using their hand-made manipulatives. The kindergarteners were enthralled when they heard a story like this:

> My new dog Elsie loves to eat everything. My mom bought a
> box of cookies. There were eight cookies in the box. Elsie ate
> two of them. How many were left?

After time had passed I clapped my hands, and each kindergartner proceeded one desk to the right. This progression would occur three times if there appeared to be enough interest between the two groups. We certainly underestimated this level of interest. . .we could have held our event all morning! The first graders demonstrated what natural teachers children can be. Every child in both classes had a wonderful experience.

To an untrained eye, our Subtraction Fair may have looked and sounded like a bunch of children playing with math at school. However, this event allowed the children in my class the opportunity to repeatedly demonstrate and explain a mathematical concept that they were attempting to solidify. As I roamed through the fair and listened to stories and explanations, I found it very easy to assess each student's grasp of the concept of subtraction. In fact I learned more that day than when I had used commercially produced material to test my students' knowledge of subtraction.

Ann Watson Cohn, Grade 1

From day one, the reading of good books is an integral part of my first-grade classroom. Children hear stories, read them, act them out, and respond to them in ways that are limited only by their imaginations. Well-written stories have the power to create reality through finely detailed settings and characters. Children willingly suspend disbelief when a new book is opened, and for the moment, accept the contents as real.

It was my goal last year to make math as integral a part of my classroom as reading. Specialists in child development agree that children in the primary grades learn best when that learning comes from their own interests and questions and is done in a real setting (Bredekamp 1987). Math educators also agree that an "essential component of what it means to understand an operation is recognizing conditions in real-world situations that indicate that the operation would be useful in those situations" (NCTM 1989, 41). With these sources providing the theoretical foundation, the argument in favor of math instruction grounded in meaningful situations was strong, but in practice, I found it hard to continually discover "real contexts" that fit naturally into my curriculum. However, in a classroom, real contexts can include situations that provide a realistic, as well as real, setting for the problem. A key is that there must be a "background" or framework for the instruction and that it be meaningful to the children. It is in answer to this need that math and literature meet.

If the world of a well-constructed children's book is part of a child's real world, then why not use it to develop children's understanding and learning of math concepts? Some books have math embedded in them as a natural part of the story. These lend themselves to problem solving, creative dramatics, and students' variations on the original. One of the first projects that combined math and literature involved the book *Anatole Over Paris* by Eve Titus. In the story, Anatole, the mouse, and his family are caught on a kite floating over Paris. In order to be rescued, Anatole instructs his brood to "turn out your pockets!" A most "curious collection" of objects results, including "two lollipops, four bottle tops, six lemon drops, eight candy cats, and a squashed chocolate éclair." Resourceful Anatole puts it all together to bribe a bird into helping the mice down to earth. That passage was an example of math in action. And the children noticed it!

Unlike traditional story problems, which tend to be simplistic, one mathematical situation in a story may develop several math concepts. This can be used to help students move from one framework of thinking to another, which I did when I used the Anatole story to further their understanding of addition. The children immediately wanted to know how many things were in the curious collection. We discussed how we might find out. One child suggested we draw each thing and count them all, and after some consideration the class agreed to this proposal. I asked them "How are we going to decide who will draw which object?" Immediately the children started volunteering to draw their favorite objects. I wrote the children's choices on the board. In short order we had a long list of names and objects. Clearly they had not yet noticed that the objects were described in groups. At this point I asked them how we could assign the drawing so that we could be sure that we accounted for all the items. We read it again and after a moment one girl suggested we "get two (children) to draw lollipops, and four to do bottle caps." Other children eagerly interrupted to add the number needed of each of the other objects. They were thinking in terms of groups! The curious collection was drawn and counted in due course. Though only a few of the children added the sets together automatically, most of them placed their carefully drawn object in the pile with like objects.

The richness and cadence of the language in stories catches the attention and imagination of children. Their delight in repeating words and phrases creates a natural reason for returning to the story and the mathematics inherent in it. In that episode in *Anatole Over Paris*, the phrases, "Sailors, empty your pockets" and "curious collection," caught my students' fancy. I used this interest to help reinforce the addition concept. On the second day I asked the children to bring two types of objects for a curious collection. The children dramatized the section of the story with strident calls to "empty your pockets." Groups of like objects were combined, added up, then put together with other objects to see what might be used to bribe the helpful bird. Each group ended with an elaborate story of its own.

Through the language of the story, the children had begun to elaborate and use their own language to explain the mathematical event that was happening in the tale. It was natural that we write these down. The third day was spent with the children in pairs, combining their curious collections and writing new endings to Anatole's adventures. In doing so they named the number and type of objects in each group, what they did with them, and how many they had in all. Matthew and Erin wrote, "Matthew and Erin turned out their pockets. Matt had one deck of cards and Erin had seven crayons. We put them together and had eight things. We offered the taxi driver eight things to take us home. And he did."

Jean Shutler, Grade 2

Oral language weaves together all areas of the curriculum in many of our classrooms. This oral language occurs when children talk to one another individually, share their thoughts with the class as a whole, initiate a discussion with a teacher, or respond to questions posed by that teacher. Historically mathematics has emphasized precise, written answers. Largely due to the focus summarized by the NCTM standards, we now realize the importance of allowing and encouraging children to verbally articulate their mathematical thinking and reasoning. There is almost always more than one way to arrive at a particular answer and occasionally more than one acceptable solution. I have found that children's understanding of math processes and concepts is enhanced through the verbalization of their thoughts. In addition, talking through a problem and making sure that everyone understands can improve basic verbal skills.

I knew that I had a terrific group of oral problem solvers very early in the year. We began our year with a curriculum focus on folk tales. In late September, we began studying the tales of that wonderful African trickster spider, Anansi. We took many scientific excursions to search for spiders and their webs. These outside walks proved to be extremely profitable, and the children saw many arachnids that they wanted to capture and bring back to the classroom for further study. For a short period of time, I was able to borrow from a colleague a wooden spider frame to house our eight-legged creatures, but the children very much wanted to have their own classroom frame.

The size and shape of a spider frame is unimportant as long as the bottom is completely submerged in water, thus creating a moat which extends twenty to thirty centimeters beyond the frame. The spiders are confined to their wooden island. Because they are unable to escape, they spin their webs, catch their prey, and attach their egg sacs for all to see. With the borrowed spider frame in the center of a seated circle of children, we discussed how we could go about solving the construction challenge of building our own. My emphasis at this point was in *how* they were going to solve the problem rather than the solution itself. Our discussion centered on what needed to be accomplished and I made sure that everyone understood the intended goal. The children decided that they wanted to work in cooperative groups and proceeded on their own to come up with various plans of action. They spent approximately twenty minutes discussing the problem, presenting their various ideas to one another, supporting or refuting the ideas of others within their group, and finally reaching a consensus to be presented to the entire class. Their solutions were varied and touched upon several of the strategies recommended to organize thinking and solve math process problems. One group wanted to *guess* the lengths of the boards used in our sample frame, unconcerned with how or if the various lengths would meet. Another wanted to measure all the lengths and make an *organized list* of what lengths were required. One group wanted to *draw a picture* of the frame so that we could copy it. The last group, which included the son of a tailor, wanted to make a paper pattern of the frame and use the pattern to measure the various lengths of wood.

The teacher plays an important part in facilitating oral problem solving. The environment that is established is very important. Providing an atmosphere that is accepting, encouraging, stimulating, and nonjudgmental will usually result in children who are willing to share their ideas. Initial small-group discussions appear to dissipate most of the feelings of anxiety. After posing any question, the teacher needs to pause several seconds or more to allow everyone the chance to *think* before answering. The teacher needs to model the acceptance of all answers. Even "wrong ideas" can contribute toward a successful solution. The teacher needs to demonstrate good listening skills and reinforce and encourage good listening attitudes in the children. The teacher needs to help the children clarify their ideas. Most of the time, if the teacher doesn't understand an idea, the rest of the class will be equally lost. Probing interjections on the part of the teacher further encourage the children to keep thinking and verbalizing their ideas. Some probing interjections would be: "Can anyone say that in a different way?" "Does anyone else have a different idea?" "Do you agree with Tommy?" "Why or why not?" "O.K." "Uh huh."

Ideally, oral math problem solving should always have a meaningful purpose for the children. Especially in the primary grades, numerous situations occur every week that could be the focus of group problem solving (such as the building of a spider frame). Allow the children to deal with the problems that teachers automatically solve.

For example, "How can we figure out if we have enough time to do this particular activity? How do we know how much string is required so that everyone can make a mobile like this one?"

Jane Moore, Grade 3

Journal writing is common practice today in elementary school classrooms. Students often write daily, filling notebooks with compositions, poetry, dialogues with teachers, and assigned essays. The phenomenon called "writing across the curriculum" took educators by storm, and many wonderful projects combining social studies, science, and literature evolved. Writing about mathematics in a journal is an effective way to see children's understandings of a concept while furthering their understanding. In addition, the math journal presents to the teacher a method of instructional evaluation. Through the journal entry, the teacher is able to gauge the impact of math activities and understandings.

I found that by using questioning techniques in response to student writing, even students having difficulties could converge on an understanding. I began with a unit on time by assigning the topic, "Why do we use the terms 'half past' and 'quarter till' when we tell time?" The results were quite fascinating. One third grader said, "Half past means, say I said half past 11:00. I mean 11:30 because there are 60 minutes in an hour. Break it in two—you've got 30." Other children needed to be coaxed through questioning toward an understanding, as shown in Figure 1.

When student journals are unclear, my questions help the authors clarify their ideas. Personal interaction between teacher and student helps children refine their thinking and sharpen their understandings. Following this journal topic, we folded paper circles, marked like clock faces. Children were instructed to match the three to the nine, make the edges even, and then fold the clock in half. After we agreed that the clock face was, in fact, folded in halves, we folded again to make four equal pieces, or fourths. The children were next asked to give another name for "fourth" and someone volunteered "quarter." Then we asked if the "half hour" and "quarter to" phrases made any sense. Some of the children who were unable to articulate this earlier in the journals were better able to understand it using the paper clocks.

Not only do journals provide an opportunity to test mathematical understanding, but they also give children chances to use imagination and creative writing. During a study of fractions, a third grader wrote

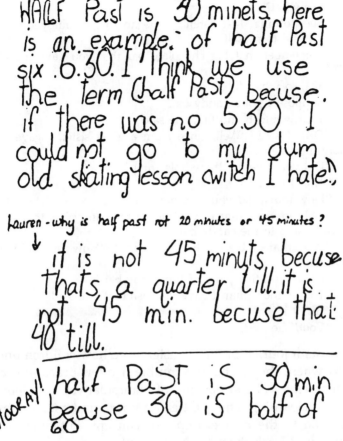

Figure 1. A sample from the mathematics journal of one of Jane Moore's third-grade students.

the following journal entry to answer the question, "Why is five-eighths bigger than one-half?"

"Because," I said. "What are we talking about?" said my little brother.

"We are talking about the fact that five eighths is bigger than one half."

"Why is it bigger?" he asked.

"Because!" I shouted.

"OK, OK, OK," said my little brother, "but I still do not understand why it is bigger," he said.

"OK, I will tell you."

"Good."

"You see," I began.

"See what?" he said.

"See nothing. Just listen" (I began to get annoyed.) "OK now," I said to myself.

"Remember that big chocolate bar that you gave me half of?"

"Yea, so what?"

"Suppose I got a candy bar."

"That would be no fair," he said.

"OK," I said. "Well, since I am a good sister, I gave you more than a half."

"Did you give me the whole thing?"

"No," I said.

"How much did you give me?" he said.

"Well, pretend that it was such a big candy bar that there were 8 parts to the candy bar."

"Wow, that's a big candy bar," he said. "How much did you give me?"

"I gave you five parts of the candy bar."

"That is more than I gave you, isn't it?" he said.

"Yes, it is."

"Cool," he said.

The math journal provides insight into how children understand math and where they're having trouble. I often prepare a lesson on a given mathematical concept, full of manipulatives, problem solving, and hands-on learning. The children appear to understand the process, so I move on to the next example or concept. But how do *I* know that *they* know? I ask them to write about it.

I have used math journals for three years now. I have used them to check understanding of concepts and to have children explain strategies for games and problem-solving. The math journal is a change of pace for the class and for me, and has shown how young children process mathematical concepts.

Our integration of the language arts and mathematics curricula at Baker Demonstration School is by no means complete; nor is it static. We each find that as we begin a new year, we refine previous plans and extend others. New questions and journal topics appear as new curriculum areas are addressed. We offer these specific examples as a starting point for other educators who wish to begin a similar integration in their own classrooms.

References

Bang, M. 1983. *Ten, Nine, Eight.* New York: Greenwillow Books.

Bredekamp, S., ed. 1987. *Developmentally Appropriate Practice in Early Childhood Programs Serving Children from Birth Through Age 8.* Washington, D.C.: National Association for the Education of Young Children.

Burningham, J. 1980. *The Shopping Basket.* New York: Macmillan Publishing Company.

Hutchins, P. 1987. *Changes, Changes.* New York: Macmillan Publishing Company.

Lobel, A. 1970. "The Lost Button." *Frog and Toad are Friends.* New York: Harper and Row, 28–39.

National Council of Teachers of Mathematics. 1989. *Curriculum and Evaluation Standards for School Mathematics.* Reston, VA: National Council of Teachers of Mathematics.

Slobodkina, E. 1968. *Caps for Sale.* New York: Harper and Row.

Titus, E. 1961. *Anatole Over Paris.* New York: McGraw-Hill Book Company.

Viorst, J. 1987. *Alexander, Who Used to Be Rich Last Sunday.* New York: Macmillan Publishing Company.

3 Talking about Babies and Ice Cubes: What Children and Teachers Do with Ideas and Language

Mary H. Maguire and Lila F. Wolfe
McGill University

Classrooms as Sites for Culture Making

Language and culture are intertwined phenomena. Both are embedded in the teaching-learning process, in what and how teachers teach, and what and how learners learn. Schools are not only instructional sites, but cultural and sociopolitical sites as well; thus, classrooms are places that offer children different opportunities for making culture and constructing knowledge. What might this mean for teachers in the elementary grades, who are usually educated as generalists but are expected to teach specialist disciplines? Should we expect different philosophies and approaches to teaching and learning language arts and science?

We open up these questions for consideration and speculation by looking in on two third-grade classroom scenarios that we observed as sites for culture making. We examine the roles of two teachers, Ms. G, teaching English language arts, and Ms. L, teaching a science lesson. What do they believe is involved in learning new ideas, particularly scientific concepts in the context of school? What role do they believe language plays in teaching children to think scientifically? What do they value as evidence of learning?

Scenario A

This is an excerpt from a group discussion of children spontaneously exploring scientific concepts through a class news-sharing routine during English language arts "lesson" in Ms. G's classroom.

C: On the news, I heard that there was a baby born without a brain and scientists don't know if he is goin' to die.

A: He's probably going to die.

B: He has a special mask and eats mushed up food. Instead of putting it down his digestive system, it goes through a cord in his belly button.

T: That's not mushed up food, that's sugar water . . . they did that to me . . . when I had my operation.

D: Yeah. My brother got that same mush when he had his ears pulled back . . . and he had to have intraviens . . . cause he couldn't drink.

T: Intravenous. Remember your sounds . . . like penis.

D: Oh!

J: How do you get that stuff?

T: They inject it right into your blood stream . . . through . . . your own . . . (inaudible)

C: If he dies they'll probably put the brain in a jar so if another baby is formed without a brain, they can make likenesses.

A: You can't do that . . . see 'cause I heard two months ago about two babies . . . were together, now, they're apart. They couldn't make it a girl and it a girl . . . they had to make it a boy and it a girl . . . you see . . . they were attached in a certain way . . . a place to they made it a girl and it a boy so they can live by themselves.

Ms. G: Oh, I see . . . I didn't hear that about the baby.

C: It was on the news and in the papers, don't you read?

A: Yeah . . . it looks like a zombie.

C: Everybody needs a brain 'cause it's connected to your nervous system.

B: If you lose your brain, you can't breathe. You don't live or want to.

Ms. G: Hum . . . that's interesting.

C: They might take a brain from a cow.

A: Look a brain from a cow is too big.

B: No A . . . the brain of a cow is too small. If you ask a cow two plus two, he couldn't answer . . . cows don't do adds.

A: No B. Wait a minute. A cow teaches her calf . . . when the calf turns into a cow . . . the calf already knows!

B: Human beings has a bigger brain than us.

D: Our brains are this big (demonstrates the size of a football).

A: Look . . . we have many things our brain has to do (stands up): see (blinks several times) . . . I just blinked . . . we do a lot more things with our brains. Look at all the things we do.

B: Yes, we can read.

D: We're even smart enough to have computers.

A: You said, we're so smart because we can talk, but a cow can talk . . . he can say moo . . . so another cow understands . . . we uh . . . all can learn a whole lot of language that way. See birds understands birds . . . cows understand cows.

T: Cows can't really communicate. The only ones are birds and dolphins.

A: Yes, a cow can communicate but maybe a cow can't communicate as much as a person.

T: Yes . . . but some scientists understand the dolphin language through sound waves under the water.

A: Look. I think we had better go to the library and find out who is telling the truth.

Here the children have used *exploratory talk*—their own everyday vocabulary—to express their ideas about certain scientific concepts. They are talking themselves into the discourse of science (Barnes 1976; Britton 1970). Their verbal expressions show what they have learned and believe about babies and other scientific concepts such as intravenous feeding, separation of Siamese twins, sound waves, and the size of brains.

Scenario B

In this class, children cluster around their desks while Ms. L circulates. As part of a lesson on the three forms of water, the children have been asked to examine an ice cube and to "Talk about how it feels. Touch it. Yes. Talk about what you're discovering about it."

Ms. L: What happened here? What's going to happen first?

B: It'll evaporate.

Ms. L: How did you know it's going to evaporate?

E: Miss, because it's water.

B: . . . liquid evaporates . . .

Ms. L: What word did you just use? Think about that word.

B: Liquid.

Ms. L: So, what's the next form of water? Do you think you've discovered the next form of water? What is it?

B: Liquid.

Ms. L: That's very good. Did you touch it? How does it feel? What words describe it?

E: Cold. Slippery.

Ms. L: What's happening as you touch it?

R: It's melting.

Ms. L: Why? Why do you think it's melting?

R: . . . it's hot.

Ms. L: So what would cause water to change from a solid to a liquid? What would it need to change?

B: Heat.

Ms. L: That's right. Very good.

Here is an example of teacher-directed *constrained talk* about ice cubes. Ms. L adopts a highly structured question-and-answer format to exercise a control over the direction of the social interaction, content of the lesson, and knowledge flow. The children attempt to negotiate the concept "evaporation," but Ms. L is looking for "liquid" as the appropriate response. Although she encourages the children to use scientific vocabulary, she focuses and directs the dialogue so that certain information evolves (*i.e.,* "ice will change from a solid to a liquid and heat is needed to do so") and certain "appropriate" terms are elicited (liquid, solid, heat).

What is going on in these conversations? Both teachers invite the children to express themselves, and both teachers are part of the discussion. Each teacher, however, plays a different role and thus creates a different cultural climate for using language and learning science concepts (Maguire 1989). The culture of a classroom is more than a physical setting; it is more than the actions and language of a teacher and children. It is the entire "context of situation," which Halliday (1978) argues involves all social interaction. This "text" includes any unit of language oral and written that is a unified whole. The conversations in the two scenarios are evidence of socially negotiated texts. But the texts involve scientific understanding.

Delamont (1983) distinguishes between "hot science," which involves genuine reasoning, observation, and experiment, and "cold science," which rests upon the uncritical reception of authoritative statements and questions (as quoted in Barnes 1988, 23). What messages are the children getting in each context? Do the conversations represent hot or cold science?

We believe the scenarios show that many things come into play in understanding the teaching-learning process, in what at first appears a relatively familiar and uncomplicated set of customary, classroom cultural activities: a news sharing routine and small group discussions on the three forms of water.

When children come to school they adapt to teachers' invitations to learn, which are usually mediated by language. In the two scenarios, we see two different educational processes and two different language registers at work. Halliday (1978) uses "register" to describe the variety of ways language is and can be used to make sense across different contexts, communities, and situations. These two classrooms are cultural communities (Maguire 1989), but are marked by different teacher assumptions, ideologies, features in routines, activities, meanings, and invitations to learn language and science concepts. Finding the link between and among the different layers of culture that impinge on teaching, learning, and classrooms as sites for culture making is complex.

Finding the Link: A Comparative Look at Teaching and Learning

Both classrooms exuded an atmosphere of joy and enthusiasm for learning and functioned as working social units. However, these two classroom cultures differed in their social organization, explicit norms, routines, and even physical space.

The thirty children in the first teacher's class, Ms. G's, were socially organized into four pods. A long table filled with children's projects sits in the middle of the room. Her desk is unobtrusive, rarely used and mostly serving as storage space for children's books, projects, and resource bins of learning tools—scissors, pens, rulers, construction paper, and tape. Ms. G circulates around the pods, the long table, and the rug area. Space in this classroom is rearranged throughout the day according to the situation.

In the second class, Ms. L's, the twenty-five children are seated in rows with her desk placed at the front of the room. The large open area, center front, is the arena from where she carries out her teaching and from where the children present their projects. Similar to Ms. G's class, books are visible everywhere: on shelves, book stands, leaning against the chalkboards, on chairs, and tables. Art work and written pieces are displayed on the walls. All types of print material are available to the children and appear to have been chosen with their interests in mind.

These classroom cultural artifacts, such as books and projects, are used in different ways and for different purposes in these two classrooms. Usually, Ms. L organizes the learning events in her classroom in two-act sequences: she presents a class lesson on a topic, such as animals, and then assigns projects from which the children can choose. Each child is expected to present an individual project. Ms. L encourages children to use their own words and not copy from the resource books that are plentiful and accessible to them. Although it may not appear as if she coerces or dominates the children's thinking, there is no doubt from the social organization of her classroom and her use of language that Ms. L is in control. This control enables her to influence and regulate the direction that talk and work takes, ensuring her objectives are fulfilled. In Ms. G's class, projects arise out of the children's conversations and interests. Her rules are explicit; the children are expected to work collaboratively, "make intelligent choices" and "use their heads." They are free to talk, move around the class; they are "in charge of organizing their projects, choosing their own books and are expected to be responsible."

In both classrooms, the children are expected to listen to whoever has the floor. Observations of both teachers confirm that they create climates conducive to children's language and learning through positive social interactions and clear and consistent goals. In Ms. L's class, we frequently hear her say "Let's listen. It's polite. Fair is fair." In Ms. G's class, we frequently hear her say "Use your head, you know the rules; you are responsible." The most explicit cultural sign of Ms. G's classroom culture is the sign on the door of her classroom that reads: *Welcome to a Creative Existence: What are you going to make of it?* The pattern of social interaction varies from child-child interactions, individual child interactions, teacher-child and teacher-children interactions. The community is defined and leadership is shared by the children and herself as co-explorers. In Ms. L's class, the dominant patterns of social interactions are teacher with children and individual children to the whole group, and this is accomplished through her favorite teaching style, a teacher-led classroom discussion. An explicit cultural signal of the children's perceptions of Ms. L as "teacher in charge" is the consistent way in which the children address her as "Miss." ["Miss" is the equivalent of "Ma'am" in traditional U.S. classrooms.] She sets the norm for appropriate language use by acting as a model, a resource for and judge of the children's use of language and thus regulates the social practices and processes in her classroom community. Why do these teachers orchestrate routines and activities in their classrooms in different ways?

Adopting a Stance/Conforming to Institutional Norms

One explanation for these two different ideologies about teaching and learning and use of language registers may be that these teachers are culturally, historically, and politically influenced to adopt a certain perspective on teaching and learning. Barnes (1976) distinguishes between two modes of teaching behavior that help children deal with knowledge—the transmission teacher and the interpretation teacher. The former believes that concepts and skills of behavior are in the public domain and are delivered to the learner by the teacher; the latter believes children acquire knowledge by organizing and reorganizing their thoughts and actions by dialoguing and working collaboratively.

Both Ms. G and Ms. L come to their classroom setting with a personal philosophy of teaching and learning. Background education and other experiences in science and teaching influence their beliefs about science and how children learn. Ms. L exhibits some of the characteristics of a transmission teacher. She presents the children with an ice cube and encourages them to talk about their observations. However, she does not see herself as a "sciency" person, and so her informational objective and teaching stance (to learn the three forms of water) prevent her from noticing how the children use various terms appropriately and in the scientific context she is attempting to create. Ms. G says she is "not just a language arts teacher for an hour and a science teacher for another hour." She does not interfere in the children's formulations of their understandings about babies born without brains, nor does she attempt to correct the information flow. As an interpretation teacher, she permits the children to feed off each other and share their prior knowledge and their understandings.

Both teachers are from second-language backgrounds and learned English and French as second and third languages in school. They now teach in Montreal schools where children are instructed in English and French. The children in both these classrooms are themselves second-language learners, English being their second language and French their third. Ms. G is quite explicit in articulating her philosophy about not correcting the children in their verbalizations, conceptualizations, and misperceptions (*e.g.*, the size of brains). She says that she is more concerned "about kids making sense out of their school experiences and making connections than correct answers." In an open-ended interview early in the school year she explains: "so don't expect to see a plan book. I plan according to what the children are doing, saying, what has gone on the day before or in the news and world and what they are talking about." She sees her role as a "facilitator of children applying their existing knowledge as they confront and reshape it to new understandings," and views "the world as a tremendous resource for children to explore and discover and change."

Ms. L is concerned about these second-language learners using correct vocabulary. She believes that all forms of reading, writing, and speaking become the vehicles for learning science and other subjects of the curriculum. She says that "some people would say that they [the children] are too young, but if they can comprehend it and if they're expanding their vocabulary, they'll get excited about learning." She believes that "language encourages them to explain things in their own words. If they can use the proper term, then all the better for them." However, she says, "sometimes I have to stop [the discussion] because we are getting carried away with discussion . . . at that moment it is very interesting and they want to share what they have discovered . . . but I don't want them to go into it too much because I don't think they have enough facts."

Not only is Ms. L influenced by her philosophy about the use of language in teaching and learning, but the culture of the school as an institution impinges on her teaching behavior. Although she believes in children's creative use of language, group interactions, and creative thinking skills, her philosophy is guided by school and institutional objectives that require students to complete formative and summative tests. This explains her need to control the direction of class discussion and her concern about children using the correct vocabulary. She explains: "Although I want the children to relate what they've learned in their lives, not just the facts, but to understand the concepts, most administrators want summative tests. So that's why the questions I was asking were specific to the things I wanted them to remember." Ms. L seems to be pulled in two different directions. On the one hand, she is concerned about the children "remembering facts" and "passing school tests." On the other hand, she believes that they learn by using writing to put down their ideas and making their own notes for peer and teacher review. This tension is reflected in the following pieces of writing, Figures 1 and 2.

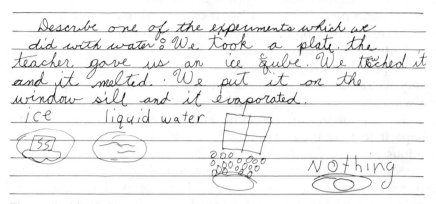

Figure 1. Maria's answer to a test question on the three forms of water.

In the first piece of writing, Maria's answers to test questions on the three forms of water are written in full sentences that state the facts she is expected to remember. However, it is interesting to see that she is guided by her own science knowledge and ideas and creates a fourth form of water—nothing! Ms. L encourages the children to make notes and embellish or explain their ideas with drawings. In the second piece, although Nadia's notes succinctly describe an understanding of condensation and evaporation, the piece reflects writing for the purpose of displaying school knowledge rather than using writing as a tool to explore and investigate ideas. However, Nadia does use a symbolic system to map out the three forms of water and their attributes.

Ms. G encourages the children to keep running records of what they are learning in spiral notebooks, as illustrated in Figure 3. In these learning logs, the children are free to make observations, lists, or charts, or to brainstorm, or to ask questions.

Thus, members of a group—a classroom community through words, gestures, written or oral texts—formulate a context and act out a context in form as well as content. We see two different subjective realities reflected in the behaviors of Ms. G and Ms. L, with each behavior socializing children to learn, talk, and write in different ways. Figure 4 provides a summary of both teachers' ideologies, perceptions, assumptions, beliefs, values about teaching and learning, language and knowledge, and talking and writing as school activities.

In relation to Barnes's characteristics of teacher ideology as transmissive and interpretive, Ms. L has some of the characteristics of

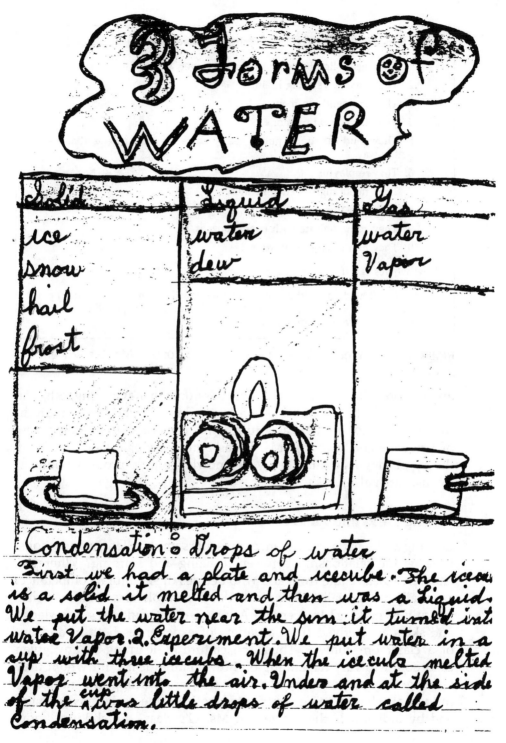

Figure 2. Nadia's answer to a test question on the three forms of water.

Some facts about whales which are obvious from this story

1. They hear slightly better under than over water.
2. They have a very big brain.
3. They are gentle to man.
4. They have good memories.
5. They send off sound pulses that bounce off solid objects that are in the way.
6. They're playful.
7. They make high-pitched sounds.
8. They will trust man.
9. They communicate with beeps, buzzes.
10. They don't like human riders.

How whales care for their young.

An (adult with or without his/her mate) will swim around with up to twelve children. When feeding adults will let children go a little way off, but will always keep in contact.

Figure 3. "The Whale Killers," a learning log by one of Ms. G's students.

an interpretation teacher, but her classroom behavior suggests she operates more in the transmission mode. Ms. G, who works more in the interpretation mode, has a functional, constructivist, dialogic view of language and learning. Ms. L has both a dialogic view and copy theory of language and theory of knowledge as a product bounded by institutional norms.

Turning Ideas into Action

Looking at the pattern differences presents some challenging questions: What is the relationship between teaching and learning? Where do children's ideas come from and who decides their cultural competence, especially in specialist disciplines? Who controls classrooms as sites for culture making? In scenario A, we see that children's knowledge and skills are derived from a variety of experiences both in and out of a classroom context. Thus, the culture of learning in any given classroom will vary depending on how children learn, for whom they perceive they are learning, and what they are learning. It is necessary to look at what is being contributed both by the social environment and by individuals themselves. In Ms. G's class, the children know

Ms. G	Ms. L
Perceives	**Perceives**
■ Teacher's task is to set up an environment with resources that children use to reshape knowledge through social interaction.	■ Teacher's role is to help students gain self-confidence as learners.
■ Teachers and children as copartners.	■ Teacher's task is to provide a stimulating environment to maintain students' sense of excitement and curiosity.
	■ Teacher should follow students' lead. Discussions are kept as much as possible within constraints of topic.
Assumes	**Assumes**
■ All children can handle whole language and make intelligent choices.	■ Children come to class with prior knowledge and experiences that should be tapped.
■ All forms of expression are acceptable.	■ Children are already eager to learn.
■ Children already have experiences and possess knowledge about the world.	
■ Children are self-motivated.	
Believes	**Believes**
■ Knowledge exists in children's ability to make choices and take sensible action.	■ Information is conveyed through discussion, reading, interacting with peers.
■ Both teacher and children have access to knowledge and skills.	■ Knowledge is gained through use of appropriate vocabulary of science and by integrating science with other subjects.
■ Knowledge is constructed.	■ Investigations should be structured to fulfill goals: success in school tests.
■ In taking an active stance for teacher change and against correcting children's work.	■ Children should be independent learners.
Values	**Values**
■ Child-centered approaches.	■ Children's use of vocabulary.
■ Children initiating, choosing, making a commitment to learning, and constructing social reality.	■ Children's involvement in discussions and preparation of projects.
■ Children working collaboratively.	■ Group work for some activities.
Thinks	**Thinks**
■ Reading and writing are processes of learning.	■ Communication skills promote understanding.

Figure 4. Summary of beliefs, assumptions and values.

that any form of discourse is ripe for exploring science, as illustrated in the following excerpt from Chris's science fiction story: "No, the martians probably created an artificial atmosphere on the planet. Ten minutes later, we were flying towards the asteroid belt."

Children bring to the teaching-learning situation certain views they have about teacher expectations, knowledge about the subject, and understandings about themselves as learners (Barnes 1976). Schwab (1962) calls this "metalearning." Language is the mediating tool in the learning process and plays a crucial role in children's understanding of ideas and ability to think scientifically. However, the differences among children in their language and learning will be influenced by the degree of mediation and control between teachers and children and their views of how knowledge and language can be or should be displayed or expressed. Children in Ms. G's class frequently engage in exploratory talking and writing and easily enter into hands-on, self-initiated investigations. For example, at the end of the news sharing routine in scenario A, the children knew the range of options they had, options that extend beyond the boundaries of the classroom. Some searched for resource books in the library; some remained behind in the rug area negotiating what they would investigate next; some looked through *National Geographic* magazines; some organized information they had gathered the day before on charts. A small group interested in the environment sat in a corner reading Shel Silverstein's book *The Giving Tree*.

Ms. L carefully plans, structures, and mediates the children's activities and learning. We see a mismatch between her philosophy of how children learn and how she invites them to learn. For example, in an interview, she states that she believes that the children "have the desire to find out all these wonderful, interesting facts about things." She says that she recognizes the need for investigations and she does organize them occasionally. However, she rationalizes her behavior by saying that the "children were quickly bored by some of the activities." She expresses her surprise and amazement when one child used scientific words in his compositions: "He uses that word [reflecting] in his openings to stories in his compositions—'While I was sitting by the river and the sun was reflecting on the water, He'll just come out of the blue with something like, you know'."

In Ms. L's class, knowledge is a commodity. Children are expected to make notes and write projects and tests, the end goal of which is that they meet the institutional criteria of the discipline of science as she perceives it within the institution of schooling. In Ms. G's class, knowledge is a constructing process and the goal is pupil participation in that process and playing with possibilities, "making connections between old and new." Children in her class know that knowledge emerges from a variety of sources, as illustrated in the following journal entry on "Vortex's."

Vortex's

I read about vortex's in D and D books. They are sort of passageways that to different planes of existence.

But mine are inter-dimensional. Everything is reversed like a mirror in the toothfairies dimension (Santa and the Easter Rabbit live there as well). That's why all three have never been seen. They can make their own vortex's in a flash, so they can appear and disappear whenever they want (or need) . . .

In the introduction of this article, we stated that elementary school teachers are usually educated as "generalists" but are expected to teach in the specialist disciplines. We raised the question: Should we expect different patterns of teaching in a science class than in a language arts class? We believe that we will continue to see different patterns emerge in teachers' classrooms as we have observed in the classrooms of Ms. G and Ms. L. However, we believe this does not necessarily need to be the case. If children learn to read by reading "real" books, would it not also be the case that children come to know science by engaging in "real" investigative activities (hot science) that encourage them to be problem seekers, problem finders, problem creators, and problem solvers. We believe that children need to engage in the culture of hot science. What can teachers do, especially teachers like Ms. L, who does not feel confident teaching science?

Teachers can orchestrate activities within a framework of trans-actions based on S. Langer's (1956) three phases of knowing: perceiving, ideating, and presenting. We see the importance in the perceiving phase when children become curious and are encouraged to confront new ideas and questions. They can do so by listening to and investigating what Freire calls the generative themes of the community, much as we see them begin to do in scenario A. In the ideating phase, we see the importance of children having opportunities for building dialogues between prior knowledge and established knowledge through listening and expressing viewpoints, searching problems, gathering, comparing, organizing, and critically evaluating information. They can do this by interviewing, making and confirming predictions about scientific events, making their own notes, and recording and comparing their observations. In the presenting phase, we see the importance of children reflecting on these experiences, transforming their understandings and turning ideas into action through some presentational form. It is this latter phase we think has been given short shrift in both language arts and science classrooms. The spirit of open-ended inquiry can be encouraged in children through their learning logs, interviewing, taping, engaging in authentic and self-initiated projects and doing what scientists do: explore, search, investigate and interpret.

Exploratory Talk and the Scientific Register

In school, many teachers perceive science to be a specialized subject with a specialized vocabulary to be transmitted to students. Some teachers, like Ms. L, think that the meaning of science vocabulary is central to understanding scientific events and often focus on the use of "correct" vocabulary—a precise use of scientific terms. Carre (1981) believes that insisting on a "specialist register" may interfere with children's learning since children construct their own meanings to terms based on their own reasoning, experiences, conceptualizations, and language. Their use and meaning may not be the same as that of scientists (*e.g.*, "skin" and "surface of liquids" versus "surface tension").

We do not believe that children should initially use precise terms when talking about science events. Rather, they should have the opportunity to act on ideas that arise, for example, when they play with and compare drops of water, vinegar, or oil. Looking back at the two conversations, we see that the children's talk in scenario A may be exploratory and imprecise but they are using language to interpret, explore, and test their ideas and they talk themselves into the scientific register by collectively pooling, comparing, and confronting their ideas.

Children's understanding of science develops as they try to make sense out of their world. Like scientists, they are curious and inquisitive and the ways they construct meaning are guided by their experiences, their prior knowledge, their use of language and opportunities for risk taking. Children's understanding of scientific events is also determined by how they learn and what kind of activities they become involved in—the act of "doing" authentic science investigations.

However, we see a profound difference between the kinds of cultures of science children are being socialized into in schools and how they learn to think scientifically. Ms. G is more concerned with encouraging and allowing the children to use language to spontaneously verbalize and construct their own understandings. However, in Ms. L's class the children's attempt to express what they know about evaporation and condensation (liquid evaporates) is redirected by her questions ("what is the next form of water") so that her institutional objective is fulfilled. How these children "talk about babies" and "talk about ice cubes" and how they learn in these two classrooms is both a pedagogical issue (what and how students learn) and a political issue (who and what controls their learning); it raises the question of what the cultural climates in classrooms might look like not only in language arts but in specialist disciplines like science.

Science teaching then includes not just learning concepts and skills nor doing investigative activities. It is also a social process that involves using language to observe, classify, compare, design an investigation, and report on results as scientists do (Wolfe 1990). Scientific understanding is promoted through dialogue, a reciprocal language and thinking process of what Polanyi (1958) calls sense reading and sense giving. Observing these two classroom teachers forced us to reshape our own assumptions about teaching and learning. Language plays a crucial role in the learning process and particularly the learning of a specialist discipline like science. Capturing what teachers and children do with ideas and language in classrooms is something we need to explore further.

References

Barnes, D. 1976. *From Communication to Curriculum.* London: Penguin.

————. 1988. "Knowledge as Action." In *The Word for Teaching Is Learning: Essays for James Britton,* edited by M. Lightfoot and N. Martin. Portsmouth, N.H.: Heinemann Educational Books.

Britton, J. 1970. *Language and Learning.* Harmondsworth, England: Penguin.

Bruner, J. S. 1986. *Actual Minds, Possible Worlds.* Cambridge, Mass.: Harvard University Press.

Carre, C. 1981. *Science.* London: Ward Lock Educational.

Driver, R. 1988. "Theory into Practice 11: A Constructionist Approach to Curriculum Development." In *Development and Dilemmas in Science Education,* edited by P. Fensham. Philadelphia: Falmer Press, 133–49.

Halliday, M. 1978. *Language as Social Semiotic: A Social Interpretation of Language.* Baltimore: University Park Press.

Hardcastle, J. 1985. Classrooms as Sites for Cultural Making. *English in Education* 19.

Langer, S. K. 1956. *Philosophy in a New Key*. New York: Mentor Books.

Maguire, M. H. 1987. Is Writing a Story in a Second Language That More Complex Than in a First Language? Children's Perceptions. *Carleton Papers in Applied Language Studies*, 29–50.

Polanyi, M. 1958. *Personal Knowledge: Towards a Post-Critical Philosophy*. Chicago: The University of Chicago Press.

Schwab, J. J. 1962. "The Teaching of Science as Enquiry." In *Elements in a Strategy for Teaching Science in the Elementary School*, edited by Brandwein, P. F. Cambridge, Mass.: Harvard University Press, 3–103.

Shor, I., ed. 1987. *Freire for the Classroom: A Sourcebook for Liberatory Teaching*. Portsmouth, N.H.: Heinemann.

Wolfe, L. F. 1990. Identifying Ideas about Science Conveyed to Elementary School Children. *Qualitative Studies in Education*, 3:15–29.

4 Creating Stories about Science through Art, Literature, and Drama

Linda Prentice
San Gorgonio High School, San Bernardino, California

Patricia Tefft Cousin
California State University, San Bernardino

The seventh grade class sits in a semicircle. Students share stories about the desert as an introductory session to our unit. Allan waits his turn to speak, and then says, "My experience with a cactus was terrible. My brother and I were chasing each other through the house. He ran out the backdoor and I followed him. What a mistake! He knocked over the prickly pear cactus and I tripped over it. Spines stuck in me everywhere! I was in pain! It hurt to take those stickers out. No one should mess with cactus! The only good thing was, I got revenge. The cactus died!"

Stories like Allan's are part of our everyday lives. We organize our world and relate to others through the use of story (Bruner 1987, 1988; Smith 1988). Yet, more often than not, when teachers enter their classrooms they ignore personal stories and rely on prepared text materials. The blending of storytelling and story writing over the day and across the curriculum is missing. Teachers sometimes forget that students need to make connections through the telling of stories as they merge their past experiences with new information they receive; they must allow the self-expression and interpretation that leads to understanding. Personal stories illustrate how most students begin to internalize new ideas and make them their own. They are the starting point for true understanding and growth.

A child's tale can be told in various ways. Children can relate a story in the ancient, oral tradition, linking themselves for the moment with other storytellers of long ago. They can draw, like the cave painters of prehistory, to convey the meaningful experiences in their lives. They can write; they can sing; they can act. And they can tell their stories through content-area subjects such as science. Storytelling covers all manner of subjects; this view takes as its central premise that "world making" is the principal function of mind, whether in the sciences or in the arts (Bruner 1987, 11).

Yet, when teaching subjects that include difficult concepts like some of those in science, teachers find themselves overwhelmed with details irrelevant to students' lives. The data are complex and teachers present them to students in a traditional manner, asking them to, say, memorize parts of a flower in order to answer questions and take tests. Students remember vocabulary words like *pistil* and *stamen* just long enough to pass the exam, yet never really grasp the near magic inherent in science. But there is a way to provide opportunities for integration of scientific notions. That avenue is through story expression. Teachers can join with students in constructing and understanding abstract concepts. We must move to an interactive level of learning where we help students integrate their prior knowledge and background experiences with the topic of study so that new and personal stories emerge. Learning occurs when the learner has a vested interest in the course of study, and not before. Success can be measured, not by a fill-in-the-blank quiz, but by stories students tell about antelope and bacteria and cells, about the living and nonliving, about galaxies and oceans.

We will share stories of how we have used art, literature, and drama as vehicles through which scientific concepts can be interpreted. We collaborated on this project in our respective roles as a public school teacher and university teacher. Our methods of collaboration vary with each project that we work on together; in this project we met biweekly and discussed effective methods for integrating science and language. Linda implemented our ideas and brought students' work back to our discussion sessions. Our analysis of their work helped us further understand the relationship between telling stories and understanding scientific concepts.

Although we believe our findings apply to all students, the classroom examples here came from a middle school science class for a diverse group of at-risk and special-needs students. We developed units on topics designated in the district's middle school science curriculum. Here we discuss two of those units, "the desert" and "the solar system."

Stories about the Desert

Our unit was part of the designated course of study, but students had freedom to choose topics of interest for in-depth study. We wanted to offer a unit that would provide a well-rounded understanding of plant and animal life in the desert, adaptation of living things in a harsh environment, and the unique ways that flora and fauna survive, particularly focusing on the deserts located in our area of Southern California.

First, we read literature that illustrated scientific concepts, for example, *Desert Giant: The World of the Saguaro Cactus* and *The Desert Is Theirs*. Another favorite was Diane Siebert's exquisitely written and illustrated work, *Mojave*. This book contains fifteen dramatic watercolor paintings by illustrator Wendall Minor that are accompanied by Siebert's lyrical prose, for example, "I see the hawk, his wings outspread. He sunward soars to block the light" (Siebert 1988, 1).

Her writing contains vivid desert images, scientific vocabulary, and figurative speech. Written language is supported by illustration. Text and art blend to create the whole. In the first activity related to *Mojave*, the students each chose a page to read and perform for the rest of the class in a reader's theater presentation. Reader's theater involves selecting a passage, reading the passage orally for practice, and then reading it in front of the class. Although it was a public performance, it was not acting per se, since there were no true rehearsals, props, or makeup. The presentation was fairly straightforward. Students usually stood in a line, stepped forward, and then read in sequence. Although we never forced fearful children to read, most initially agreed to read one or two lines, and then read full passages as we continued to use reader's theater in the class.

Our purpose in providing opportunities for reader's theater performances was to create integrated moments of learning for students. When children chose parts and performed according to their own inner visions, new interpretations were born. Students who became hawks and lizards and bats believed that science was fascinating. The intangible aspects of learning—attitude and motivation—were enhanced, and children looked forward to more.

In a related activity, we made sock puppets of the desert creatures described so beautifully in *Mojave*. Each student chose an animal or desert feature (dune, arroyo, mountain) that was personally appealing and fashioned a puppet based upon that choice. The students used the book as a guide and then drew their own tortoises, jackrabbits, tumbleweeds, ravens, and big horn sheep, which they glued to the sock. Decorative touches included glitter and paint and yarn. Some might be surprised to read about the use of puppets with young adolescents, but they read and acted out their scripts to a classroom audience whose applause confirmed their efforts.

Beyond this they wrote scripts in cooperation with a partner. Each pair invented fictional problems that needed to be worked out. For example, in one script, a tarantula encountered a scorpion and they battled to the death. The story included all the components of plot development—exposition, rising action, climax, falling action, and resolution. Each script was edited by the writers and then the teacher. We constructed a simple stage—a barrier, really, made of one classroom table perched at a right angle upon another so puppeteers could hide— and we let the performances begin. An excerpt follows:

Hawk: I see you, Mouse, under that prickly pear cactus. I need to eat you for lunch.

Mouse: If you try to get me, Hawk, you will get poked with spines.

Hawk: Oh, no, Mouse! I am powerful. Spines will not hurt me!

Mouse: Wait. I have an idea. If you promise not to eat me, I will help you find other food. Let me climb onto your back and soar through the sky with you and together we will search for food. I know where there is a barn full of grain. I will take you there.

Hawk: Alright, Mouse, it might be fun to have a friend. Let's go.

We videotaped each performance and played it back immediately. Students critiqued their performances by stating what they liked best about themselves (great puppet!) and where they thought they might improve (spoke too fast, needed a louder voice). We also discussed what we liked best about the other presentations (funny script, creative problem solving, good voice projection). Again, we succeeded in creating personal stories relevant to each student's interests, while incorporating reading, writing, listening, and speaking at the same time. In the process of writing their scripts, students articulated their current understanding of adaptation as it applied to a certain animal of the desert. Skills, in other words, were developed out of the whole, and their use in context made sense to the students.

For our culminating desert experience, we piled on a bus for a trip to the Living Desert near Palm Springs, California. There we were introduced to the flora and fauna we'd studied in books. We observed beavertail, hedgehog, and cholla cacti; we hiked to a hill of big horn sheep; we inspected rattlers and scorpions and bats. We visited Indian hogans and an aviary full of desert birds. We watched the ravens overhead, sweated in the desert heat, and rested in the shade. When we returned to school, we drew and painted our favorite parts of the trip. We shared oral stories. One story became a legend.

Allan read the map he was given by the docent. He discovered a pond he wanted to explore and insisted we all follow along. He ignored the few grumbles of his hot, sweaty classmates and trudged doggedly on. Finally, we reached a muddy, green puddle and the group sighed as our vision of a clear, blue pond evaporated. Then, suddenly, Allan cried out, "Mrs. P, Mrs. P! It's called Allan Pond!" The students clustered around a bronze plaque that confirmed Allan's announcement. Allan beamed and claimed the mudhole as his own.

This story was Allan's story and ours as well. The stories belonged to the students and to us and grew from the desire to make learning real and relevant. Through our reading, writing, and creative activities related to the desert, we provided children with memorable experiences. Allan and the others in the class built links, in their own ways, to the desert, its geologic formations, its creatures.

Stories about the Solar System

As we moved from the study of the desert to the study of the solar system, we maintained our belief that scientific concepts, when blended with art, drama, reading, writing, listening, and speaking, can be the foundation for story creation. The solar system, one area of study in the curriculum, was chosen by the students in a vote we conducted. Choice, even on this somewhat controlled level, provided students with a great degree of participation in their own learning.

Students began their literary work for this unit by participating in a "what do we know?" and "what do we want to find out?" discussion. Oral participation stimulated ideas for writing and students then wrote essays about the planets. They bound their writing into class books they had illustrated. Some children wrote about other heavenly bodies like stars, comets, and asteroids. One group studied gravity on the earth and moon, in a black hole, and in other galaxies, and then presented their findings to the class. They answered "what if" questions in cooperative groups. Such questions as "What if we had no moon?" and "What if the earth didn't rotate or revolve?" were generated in a large group discussion.

We also knew that models would be imperative. Although the solar system includes only nine orbiting planets, numerous other heavenly bodies exist in space. In our classroom, each student selected a planet or other celestial body to study, to draw, to write about, and to become during a dramatic presentation. Students read a variety of trade books to find out additional information for their project, such as, *Discovering the Stars, Five Secrets in a Box, Nightgown of the Sullen Moon,* and *Sun and Moon.* They created huge planets and asteroids and comets of paper to match their "character." These props provided visual interest and further involved the children in the creative process. Students composed stories in the first person. An example follows:

> I am the sun.
> I am the center of the solar system.
> I am a ball of burning gases.
> I give you light and heat.
> You could not live without me.
> I give you the day.
> You turn away from me at night.
> I am the sun.

The students memorized their parts. They came to the front of the class and stood in the same order as the planets. The sun first, then Mercury, then Venus, then Earth until all nine were represented. They spoke their parts, with many rehearsals, until the presentations flowed. We discussed clarity of voice, projection, inflection, enthusiasm. As the rehearsals moved along, the production improved. Finally, when oral recitations and artistic pieces were complete, we moved the whole production to the stage for videotaping.

Actors crowded the stage. The sun took her place at the center. Nine planets and other assorted galactic bodies gathered round, rotating, revolving. The sun stepped forward and began to speak. She completed her part and retreated to the center of the solar system. Mercury moved up to take center stage. He described himself and the drama played on to the end, all planets and meteorites and pieces of cosmic dust reciting lines and acting parts.

Our planetary play moved a step beyond reader's theater and encouraged further interpretation by students as they acted on cue, used props, recited memorized lines, and developed more sophisticated oral language skills. This demanding and elaborate presentation asked more from students, individually and cooperatively, yet supported our belief that learning increased in relationship to interest, experience, and participation.

After students viewed the videotape, we discussed how interactive involvement through art and drama helped them gain a greater understanding of the lessons involved. Students agreed that active involvement made science more enjoyable and easier to learn. When asked to restate concepts, the majority of students were able to satisfactorily explain, for example, the effects of revolution, how rotation affects our earth, and what would happen if gravity were lost or if the sun burnt itself out. Opportunities to use art and drawing, puppetry and drama, and oral stories and song made complex notions understandable.

Connections between science and narrative were also made through poetry. Space and the basic concepts of the solar system seemed the perfect stuff for poetry. We focused on the creation of haiku. We began our exploration of haiku with examples from three companion volumes, *Cherry Blossoms, Haiku Harvest,* and *Japanese Haiku.* The thin volumes contain hundreds of perfectly crafted poems, still beautiful centuries after they were written.

We read the poems orally for fifteen minutes or so, allowing children the opportunity to consider the themes of haiku. Traditionally, haiku reflects one's relationship with nature. Seasons are often revealed in haiku poetry by the subtle mention of symbolic words like "blossoms," "wheat," "golden leaves," "frost." We read aloud and then discussed the language to see if the students could guess what season the poem suggested. We talked about the words and the figurative language.

Rhythm, as well as theme, was an important consideration and was created through the careful counting of beats; five for the first line, seven for the second, and five for the last. Since syllables needed to be counted, there was a great deal of chin tapping and hand clapping as students measured the beats to words like asteroid and universe and Mercury. The haiku process involved all of the things included in the traditional skills approach. The difference, however, was an important one. Such things as spelling, grammar, capitalization, spacing, titles, and margins came from creating a whole text and not from ditto sheets that emphasize separate, disconnected skills.

Students wrote about the stars and moon, oxygen and atmosphere, comets and meteors. Their work reflected personal interests while fusing all components of the writing process with information on our solar system. Students successfully created clear, concisely written pieces of prose and poetry with scientific concepts as a theme. Through poetry, we illuminated planetary relationships, including rotation and revolution, seasons, and gravitational pull. Our students were able to express lyrically the basic notions of space needed for an elementary understanding of the star system.

Cynthia, one of the students in the class, demonstrated through her haiku how she integrated science into her notion of the world using reading, writing, and story.

> Tiny stars floating
> Light, star in heaven, yellow
> Distant, peaceful point
>
> Tiny bluetime stars
> Glowing points emerge at night
> Stars, burning gases
>
> Morning stars light us
> Clouds come out when stars retreat
> Stars in blackness; dark

We know that experiences such as those just discussed provide students with appropriate frameworks for organizing their experiences. Scientific concepts are linked to children's conceptions and understandings. The concepts become a part of their stories of the world. The opportunity to create narratives supports the students in connecting to science in ways most have not previously experienced. Our success was documented through the high quality of written and artistic work produced by the students and through our observation and recording of their discussion about these concepts. Previously, most of these students in this class showed little interest in science, having failed this academic area the past school year.

The use of art, literature, and drama provided the vehicles through which the students interpreted the world of science. They created their own stories. They painted, sculpted, and performed. They expressed understanding through the use of alternative sign systems. The varied symbol systems drew students into the inquiry process, supporting them as they hypothesized about the world they observed. This expression offered students a basis for subsequent interpretation through oral and written language. John-Steiner (1987), in her study of creative individuals, discovered that the process through which each interpreted the world uniquely affected the ultimate understanding of a specific concept or idea. We observed this with our students. The interpretive experiences provided in this class were critical for their understanding and created new opportunities for developing concepts about science that rarely existed before.

Moll (1990) has discussed Vygotsky's ideas about the connection between everyday and scientific concepts. Vygotsky, a Russian psychologist and scholar, believed that these two types of concepts were "interconnected and interdependent." Students interpret scientific concepts through their knowledge gained from daily experiences. This interpretive process becomes reciprocal. "Everyday concepts mediate the acquisition of scientific concepts . . . and everyday concepts . . . are mediated and transformed by the scientific concepts; they become the 'gate' through which conscious awareness and control enter the domain of the everyday concepts" (10–11). The dialectic created by linking everyday concepts and scientific concepts affects students' understanding and use of both.

A curriculum that supports students in this linkage enables them to then use scientific concepts to solve the problems of the world (Tharp and Gallimore 1988). Our students' work demonstrated that the curriculum in this class created such an opportunity. Nevertheless, such changes in the curriculum were not easy. As students and teachers, our shared history of studying science was very traditional. Yet, our observation of student engagement convinced us that our focus on creating stories about science provided one successful alternative for these students to learn about the world.

References

Bash, B. 1989. *Desert Giant: The World of the Saguaro Cactus.* New York: Little, Brown.

Baylor, B. 1975. *The Desert Is Theirs.* New York: Macmillan.

Brighton, C. 1987. *Five Secrets in a Box.* New York: Dutton.

Bruner, J. 1987. "Life As Narrative." *Social Research* 54: 11–32.

———. 1988. "Research Currents." *Language Arts* 65: 574–83.

John-Steiner, V. 1987. *Notebooks of the Mind: Explorations of Thinking.* Albuquerque, N.Mex.: University of New Mexico Press.

Moll, L. 1990. *Vygotsky and Education: Instructional Implications and Applications of Sociohistorical Psychology.* Cambridge, England: Cambridge University Press.

Pfister, M. 1990. *Sun and Moon.* New York: North/South Books.

Santrey, L. 1982. *Discovering the Stars.* Mahway, N.J.: Troll Associates.

Siebert, D. 1988. *Mojave.* New York: Thomas Crowell.

Smith, F. 1988. "What the Brain Does Well." Address presented at
     California State University, San Bernardino.

Tharp, R., and Gallimore, R. 1988. *Rousing Minds to Life: Teaching,
     Learning, and Schooling in a Social Context.* Cambridge, England:
     Cambridge University Press.

Willard, N. 1983. *Nightgown of the Sullen Moon.* New York: Harcourt Brace
     Jovanovich.

5 When Decades Collide: An Interdisciplinary Approach to Research and Technology

Kathy Mathers
Washington Irving Junior High School, Colorado Springs, Colorado

One of the nicest compliments I ever received came from a visitor who popped into my classroom one day, watched my students hard at work on a wide variety of projects, and asked, "Just what is it that you teach, anyway?" Understanding why he was puzzled, I had to chuckle, because there were so many things going on that this could have been a science or social studies class just as easily as English. One group was hard at work designing an anti-dropout advertising campaign; a second was making a video for students in our feeder schools on how to survive junior high; a third was developing a community service project on environmental issues; and yet another was composing a letter to the editor of our local newspaper arguing against the need for a teen curfew. The one thing these activities had in common was that each was language centered. Whether students were collecting research data, writing reports on interviews they had conducted, or preparing persuasive pieces, they were all synthesizing language into their interdisciplinary projects.

I must admit that I am happiest when I am wise enough to listen for cues that tell me what my students feel most passionately about. Then, I can act as facilitator, coach, and cheerleader as they take control of their own learning. Perhaps this example of a recent project best explains my philosophy.

Two years ago my teaching partner, Jim Lamphear, and I spotted an article in *USA Today* that we shared with our seventh graders. It stated that Americans have the dubious distinction of being the worst spellers in the English-speaking world, according to Gallup International, the survey firm. We were interested in their reaction to this indictment, but we were unprepared for what followed. They were incensed, to put it mildly, that once again some person or institution was taking potshots at their country. They began to catalogue, in exasperation, all the other areas in which America seemed to be losing its competitive edge. The discussion raged on heatedly for two days as they filled the boards with their concerns. It seemed incredible that we were having a dialogue of such depth with twelve-year-olds! Ali summed it up for the group when she observed, "We need to become part of the solution, not just for ourselves but for our children; we need to provide a legacy of excellence instead of mediocrity."

As their comments continued to flow, we realized that we were perhaps on to something significant. At that moment "The Project" was born, and our students embarked upon a year-long examination of what they identified as the six major problems that plague our nation: we were once pacesetters in the automotive industry; we were once leaders in the electronics field; we were once known as the best educated people on earth; we once boasted of the finest health care systems in the world; we were once the keyholders to space; and we were once unrivaled in scientific research and technology.

Clearly, our students felt threatened by this perceived erosion of our global stature. Because they feared that what is occurring today could well have a devastating impact on their futures, they decided that they would not be content to produce a superficial and noncommittal report. Rather, they set out to define the present situation, examine and delineate the causes, and finally, suggest solutions.

From the start, it seemed important that we make the attempt to bring our students in contact with the most current technology, resources, and experts available. To increase the number of our contacts, we turned to parents. We suggested various ways for them to get involved:

- Did they have a computer with a modem and access to bulletin boards or information services?
- Would it be possible for our students to use their long distance phone services or fax machines to send or receive information?
- Could they put students in contact with individuals who were experts in their field, either via letter or phone or, preferably, in person?
- Did anyone have a connection with NASA or other space-related agencies whose research and development was on the cutting edge?

- Could anyone help us make a contact with a prominent scientist, engineer, executive, economist, author, educator, futurist, or government official?

- How else might we bring our students in contact with experts around the world?

- Could anyone arrange to have the students' final reports professionally typed, printed, and bound into a book?

- Would anyone's company be willing to underwrite trips for onsite interviews, observations, meetings, or conventions?

- Because we had a compelling need for more computers, did anyone work for a company that was about to replace or update its computer system and might be willing to donate old computers, printers, modems, or software to our school?

Once we allowed ourselves to look beyond the obvious requests teachers usually make of parents, we learned Important Lesson #1: THINK BIG. Did it sound as if we were asking for the moon? We were! But we were willing to take the risk because we wished to instill in our students the belief that one's passion, drive, and efforts can truly make a difference.

It didn't take long before we had "hooked" a group of parents who shared our vision. Not only did they help us make some important contacts, but they also found many more ways to help:

- They arranged visits to several companies in our area.

- They served as mentors for students who needed help generating ideas, locating information, and understanding what they were reading.

- They accompanied us on field trips.

- They supervised a variety of classroom activities at school.

Observing that these parents, many of whom were busy people, seized the opportunity to share our passion, excitement, and commitment, we learned Important Lesson #2: MOBILIZE YOUR PARENTS. Because we had the good sense to tap this valuable source of help, we were soon on our way to achieving our goals.

Once our students had settled into their groups, we presented a variety of note-taking methods, encouraging each to try the method that seemed to best suit his or her learning style. Together, we began looking for articles that illuminated the problem, and almost overnight students collected enough to fill every inch of bulletin board space in our rooms. To each article they attached an index card stating the main idea they had identified. It seemed clear that we would have a rich supply of material with which to work.

We encouraged each student who had a VCR to set aside a tape especially for the project and to be on the lookout for documentaries, specials, and relevant spots on the local and national news. Soon we had a burgeoning supply of clips from such diverse sources as ABC's "Nightline," "American Agenda," and "20/20"; CBS's "60 Minutes," "48 Hours," and "Sunday Morning"; NBC's "Meet the Press" and "Sunday Today"; and a variety of PBS offerings.

As we soon learned, the timing could not have been more perfect for a project of this nature. George Bush, our "Education President," called the governors together for an education summit in the fall. Our own governor, Roy Romer, soon after announced his own plan of action for revitalizing education in Colorado and set up a series of town meetings that we attended. The "Big Three" automakers fought to recapture their market share as Japanese cars replaced them in the hearts—and driveways—of American consumers. Japanese electronics firms continued to produce well-made, durable, and appealing products as American companies struggled to create new quality control measures. Japanese businessmen chose to invest in America with their new-found wealth, buying significant chunks of real estate all over the country. Proponents for a national health care system proclaimed its wisdom and necessity if America hoped to deliver equitable health care to all at an affordable price. NASA's leaders took some small steps but stumbled in their attempt to regain their pre-*Challenger* position of preeminence in the space race, as other countries continued to close the gap.

As our students' research progressed, we made efforts to expose them to as many experts as we possibly could. We are fortunate to live in a community that is home to a number of high-tech companies; consequently, our parents were able to put us in contact with executives at Cray Computer, Digital, and Hewlett Packard. Initially, these people merely offered to show our students around their plants assuming, perhaps, that that would be the extent of a twelve- or thirteen-year-old's interest. This led us to Important Lesson #3: CLEARLY STATE YOUR NEEDS. In each case, we stressed that our students did not want or particularly need a tour of the facilities. Instead, it was vital that these visits center around discussions with individuals who could not only provide pertinent information but discuss their evolving theories and solutions with them as well.

Time after time, our young researchers amazed the experts by sharing their insights with them. The ability to discuss real issues in an informed manner was, without a doubt, one of the most empowering experiences students gained from the entire project. Thus, we learned Important Lesson #4: MAKE SURE YOUR STUDENTS ARE WELL-PREPARED. The wisdom of this lesson was driven home to us repeatedly as we listened to them hold their own in conversations with engineers, astronauts, CEOs, school superintendents, physicians, and members of the media. What confidence and poise they displayed!

While we were fortunate enough to have so many resources conveniently at hand, let me emphasize that this is not a prerequisite to obtaining help from people in high places. It might take you a bit longer to "click" with the right person but, by all means, do attempt to make these contacts by phone or mail. Your public library's information center can probably provide you with addresses, phone numbers, and sometimes even names. Herein lies Important Lesson #5: DON'T OVERLOOK OBVIOUS RESOURCES. We made friends with a reference librarian and found her to be extremely helpful.

Let me also suggest that you keep your own vertical files of news and magazine articles, pamphlets, etc., on subjects that could be of potential interest to your classes. If I spot the name of a spokesperson, or get an idea about how to make a contact, I highlight it for future reference. On many occasions such articles have helped me to compose an intelligent, to-the-point letter that might otherwise have been dismissed as just another generic request for help. This, then, is Important Lesson #6: KEEP TRACK OF POTENTIAL RESOURCES.

Over the months, we had a variety of experiences that helped our students focus on the issues. One day, after meeting with one of our research groups, a marketing and communications executive for Hewlett Packard helped us achieve our first real coup. When we mentioned how frustrating it was for us to conduct a program of this scope that required access to technology and phone lines that are an essential part of each business but unattainable luxuries to a school district, he shrugged his shoulders and asked what we needed. Within days he had arranged a teleconference with an executive in Japan.

A snowy day in February began with a call from a CBS News producer who had managed to ferret out the story of our kids and their undertaking. "What's going on there? Tell me more about this project," he prompted us, announcing that the network might be interested in featuring us in an upcoming documentary. And we were reeling!

From this point, one success led to another. The Colorado Medical

Society rewarded our medical group for information they uncovered in the *Congressional Record* by purchasing a special slide presentation for their use. After seeing an outline of the recommendations that grew from our investigations, they invited the seven members of the group to present their findings at their annual spring conference in Denver. As our students delivered their reports, Jim and I carefully studied the reactions of this distinguished audience, which ranged from nods of agreement to amazement at such wisdom, to disgruntlement as our fact finders occasionally touched a nerve. At the luncheon that followed, our young researchers gleefully heard the keynote speaker, Governor Romer, convey item-for-item virtually the same messages and cautions that they had just delivered! Chatting with our students afterward, more than one physician shook his or her head in wonder at the precociousness of these junior high students.

Upon learning that the National Space Symposium would be held locally at the Broadmoor Hotel, we made contact with the director of education for the U.S. Space Foundation seeking permission to bring our space group to hear Vice President Dan Quayle's address. Due to the security nightmare that accompanies the appearance of such a VIP (plus the fact that the tickets cost several hundred dollars!), we were told "No." Then, several days prior to the symposium, something happened that truly caught us off guard. In our building it is uncommon for a teacher to be summoned to the office to accept a phone call, but I knew it was an uncommon day indeed when the school secretary buzzed me on the intercom to inform me that I had a call from the White House! My students roared with laughter. Who was playing a practical joke on their perpetually gullible teacher? But, indeed, it was the White House calling. It seems that our persistent requests had attracted the attention of not only the vice president but also Dr. Mark Albrecht, the executive secretary of the National Space Council. This was Mr. Quayle's secretary calling to tell us how intrigued he was with our project. By the next day, our students were not only scheduled to hear the vice president, but also to meet with Dr. Albrecht, who was equally fascinated. Both have junior-high-aged children, and both wanted our students to know how impressed they were with the commitment they were making to their future.

During our visit to the Space Symposium the seven members of our space group—the only students in attendance—were bombarded with questions by members of the press and a host of key figures in the space industry, all of whom seemed genuinely interested in what we were doing there. We listened with pride as our students confidently discussed their research with astronauts, reporters, NASA representatives, and a project manager from the Jet Propulsion Lab.

This experience led to numerous opportunities such as participation at a local schoolhouse meeting and a presentation before the state board of education, not to mention interviews for radio talk shows, television newscasts, and a variety of newspapers and magazines including *USA Today* and *Spacewatch*. A metamorphosis was taking place in our students. They had begun to realize, with good reason, that they truly had something significant to say, and that prominent people all over the country were sitting up and taking notice.

We were pleased that our kids were not intimidated by these experiences; in fact, they had acquired so much knowledge that they were eager to participate in an honest exchange of information. There was Corinne, who spoke convincingly on the great need for parity in the schools; John, who patiently explained the merits of paternalism in Japanese businesses; and Julie, who so articulately argued NASA's need for augmented funding.

Everyone in our school seemed to be enjoying this blitz of press and publicity as much as we were. I worried momentarily that students in my other classes might feel left out or even jealous of all the attention our research groups were receiving, but as it turned out I didn't need to worry. I will never forget the day my most "challenging" student brought his best friend to meet "my teacher who talked to the White House!"

As our confidence level rose, we accelerated our letter-writing campaign. Together we wrote almost 150 letters to everyone from CEOs to President Bush, succinctly outlining the project and asking for something specific. Acknowledging that these were busy people we were contacting, we practiced Important Lesson #7: LIMIT ALL CORRESPONDENCE TO ONE PAGE. Besides, we figured the odds were better that someone would actually read our letters if we did. For whatever the reason, we scored more often than not. As a result, we were able to involve our students in conference calls with CEOs of international companies, analyze data on "concept cars" of the future provided by auto magnates, view video reports prepared for board meetings, meet with astronauts and space engineers, and share a host of other opportunities.

Every time we had a request granted, we made a point to respond promptly with thank-you letters, both from us and from the students. Sometimes we would receive a follow-up letter or phone call commenting on how pleased the individual was to learn specifically how our students were making use of the information he or she had provided. One thing would sometimes lead to another, and often we received more than we had requested. We knew one thing: We had managed to capture the attention of a number of influential people and get them excited about what our kids were doing. We were amazed and gratified that so many busy executives were not only willing, but actually anxious, to help us. This realization led to Important Lesson #8, which was to become our philosophy: IF YOU DON'T ASK, YOU DON'T GET.

While our successful contacts far outweighed the not-so-satisfying ones, there were some people who politely declined to help us. Sometimes, granted, these negative responses were in answer to some of our more audacious requests: "Sorry, no, we are unable at this time to send you and your students to Japan"; or "The president of our company regrets that he will not be available to meet with your students when he visits Colorado later this month due to the fact that his agenda is already full." Actually, this feedback was usually not a firm "no" as much as it was a reminder to us that we had to anticipate our needs and plan ahead. Important Lesson #9, then, is this: BE SURE TO ALLOW PLENTY OF LEAD TIME TO ENSURE THE MOST SATISFACTORY FULFILLMENT OF YOUR REQUESTS. We'll never know how far we might have gone with this project if only we had realized this sooner.

Sprinkled in with our numerous successes were some real ironies that alternately vexed and amused us. A prime example centered around our many attempts to reach the CEO of one of the American automotive companies, an intriguing individual for whom our auto group had some rather pointed questions:

- Does the human tendency to resist change play a role in the struggle to convince the public to again buy American cars?
- How can the American automakers create an atmosphere within their companies that will foster a more loyal and enthusiastic work force?
- Why aren't the millions of dollars spent on advertising bringing about the increased sales the auto makers desire and need?
- In what ways do American cars equal or surpass Japanese autos in quality?

Unfortunately, the public relations representative of this company informed us that the CEO was far too busy to speak to the students or even to respond to them in a letter, but he wished us good luck with our project. Then, after watching a "Nightline" segment featuring Thomas Elliott, the top American official with the Honda Corporation, we wrote to him with a similar request. To our surprise, his office responded promptly that he would be happy to help in any way he could. One of the highlights of the project turned out to be a lengthy conference call between Mr. Elliott and our auto group.

There was yet another lesson we stumbled upon quite by accident, and it yielded good results even in some cases where people we contacted couldn't meet or speak with us directly: Important Lesson #10 is this: REQUEST THAT EVERYONE YOU CONTACT SEND INDIVIDUAL LETTERS TO THE STUDENTS. Because most of our research groups only numbered six or seven, this request did not seem out of line. Individuals who were nice enough to respond included CEOs of auto companies, directors of space-related agencies, and presidents of medical societies. In addition, because we were beginning to attract a good deal of local, state, and even national attention, we requested—and received—letters for each student from our superintendent and other key administrators, various elected officials, the governor of our state, and even Vice President Quayle and President Bush!

We learned something rather interesting from this process, too. Important Lesson #11 is this: KEEP CAREFUL RECORDS OF YOUR CONTACTS, AND LET ONE CONTACT LEAD TO ANOTHER. For example, we found that one White House secretary could provide us with certain information, but she would need to refer us to someone in an entirely different office to grant another request. You should see our Rolodex!

In some cases, especially as the end of the year approached, we had to ask more than once. Our efforts paid off in a big way, though, thereby helping us learn Important Lesson #12: BE POLITE BUT PERSISTENT. I wish you could have seen our students' faces when we presented each with a shiny red folder containing those letters. Be assured that most of them are carefully preserved in scrapbooks or document frames.

When we plunged into this project, Jim and I were certainly correct in recognizing that we wouldn't be able to pull it off without some serious help from a variety of sources. We were also correct in assuming that our students were capable of producing high-quality, in-depth reports. The challenge we posed to them was to synthesize the various recommendations they had collected into their own creative solutions to cure America's ills. We had kept close tabs on them all year, both individually and in their groups, through weekly work logs, periodic summaries of work-in-progress, and meetings with the groups. We optimistically expected the papers to be excellent, and we were terribly impressed with the quality work completed by these motivated students. In fact, easily one-third of the papers surpassed even our highest expectations and standards.

We were deeply moved in our realization that students, even twelve- and thirteen-year-olds, can think and understand and make an impact on their society. These students are symbols—symbols that all students of all abilities can attain great heights if the interest is piqued, the encouragement is given, and the essential help is available. Our goal was to provide our students with the most significant undertaking of their lives and, from their very candid critiques, we seem to have accomplished that goal.

> I guess I have never been pushed or pushed myself to this extent before. Only when I was typing my final report did I begin to realize how much I had learned.
>
> —Veronica

> When I finished the report it hit me: I'm an expert at something and I feel confident talking to anyone about it.
>
> —Jennifer

> This project has been so fulfilling, especially when I realize that I probably know more about the auto industry than 90 percent of the people in this country. I now know that my limitations are not those of a normal seventh grader.
>
> —David

> I pushed and I struggled and I found this project wasn't about a grade, but something much more important. Not only did I learn a lot about writing and long term commitments, but I now have an authoritative understanding of why the U.S. is not living up to its potential, and what my generation can do about it.
>
> —Missy

Jim and I probably learned more from this experience than our students. For one thing, it confirmed our theory that the more actively engaged students are in their work, and the more opportunities they have for actually selecting what they study, the more they will feel they own the material. We learned how to help them analyze, investigate, question, challenge, and draw conclusions. We learned how important it is to act as a coach, not merely a disseminator of information. We learned to give students ownership of their futures.

Had it been worth the incredibly long hours, the intense brainstorming sessions, the often painful process of helping our students make sense of material that was so difficult to comprehend? Absolutely! How many times do teachers have the opportunity to shape the future in such a concrete way? From our students' assessment of what the project had meant for them, it seemed clear to us that we had nurtured a group of future decision makers who would be prepared to assume leadership roles in society, the family, and the work place. These were students who would never be content to merely sit back and watch things happen.

And so, despite the many woes that plague America, there are kids, and especially our thirty-five seventh graders, who can and have gone beyond expectations held by teachers, parents, and society. America's future is in good hands. Students just need a push, a cause, someone to believe in them, direction and guidance, an occasional pat on the back, and—in this case—two normally quite sane and rational teachers. By being willing to take a few risks, by responding to our students' needs, by rewriting the curriculum as we went along, and by following our instincts, we were able to lead our students on a pretty amazing journey that none of us will ever forget.

6 Students and Their Teacher Talking in the Middle School Science Classroom: What Does Their Discourse Mean?

Pamela Sissi Carroll and Alejandro J. Gallard
Florida State University

Two seventh graders are talking as they lean over a map:

> "You can't say that that hurricane is going to start there!"
> "Why not? He said that a hurricane wiped out a lot of land and houses in Tallahassee a few years ago."
> "That's right, but it didn't *start* here. We're too far north. And we aren't in the middle of the ocean."
> "Oh yeah. You're right. I guess I better move it."

How do scientists share information, negotiate interpretations, construct knowledge? They talk. They argue. They influence other scientists and nonscientists through verbal persuasion like Plato, Bacon, Priestley, and Darwin did. In "Rhetoric of Science" (Harris 1991, 282–307), R. Allen Harris provides a clear outline of connections between the domains of science and rhetoric. Harris calls scientists "rhetors" who "make knowledge through mutual suasion" (295) and defines rhetoric of science as "the study of suasion in the interpretation of nature" (284). He justifies attention to rhetoric of science as a field of inquiry by grouping the genre with two other studies of science: (1) sociology of science, which studies scientific communities and their relation to societal pressures, and (2) psychology of science, which studies the cognitive processes that lead to the "generation and promulgation of scientific ideas" (287) and the relation of the processes to psychological issues in general. Harris argues that the recent development of "a specific genre of rhetorical analysis directed at scientific discourse" (282) must be assigned a place within the context of other studies of science. No teacher, regardless of subject area specialty or level of instruction, can ignore the necessity of language—of rhetoric and discourse—in our classrooms. Language is the means through which we are able to make and share meaning as we work toward construction of knowledge.

The rhetoric of science focuses on the role of discourse, especially verbal persuasion, as it is used for "galvanizing, resolving, or avoiding disputation" (Harris 1991, 287). Therefore this genre, like sociology and psychology of science, is concerned with approaches scientists take in sharing information.

We have attempted to study rhetoric of science in a setting that is replete with examples of science discourse: one teacher's middle school science classes. Our perspectives, even upon entering the classroom, are different, because one of us is a science educator and the other is an English educator. But we share a philosophic stance: we believe that the most successful teachers are those who help students learn to question and to reflect on their experiences and observations in order to construct knowledge for themselves. Such teachers do not dominate the classroom with insistence that students learn a specific collection of predetermined, previously articulated facts; instead, their goal is for students to *think* as well as to *know*. We believe, too, that interdisciplinary approaches enhance learning.

This study is interpretive. We were welcomed into the sixth- and seventh-grade classes of a twelve-year teaching veteran. We used video cameras, field notes, interviews of teachers and students, classroom observation, reviews of artifacts such as tests and students' journals, and participation with small groups of students in order to gather data one day each week. We met to discuss what we were seeing and thinking after each observation/interview period and before the next visit. This routine provided a framework for making sense of what we had seen, recorded, and reflected upon during each class, and it offered insights for observations during subsequent classes.

Our purpose was to investigate the role that language plays in the teaching and learning of science in middle schools. We were especially interested in listening to teacher-student and student-student interaction. As our study progressed, we became interested in three related questions. How does the teacher use vocabulary to explain science phenomena? Do students learn to mimic and then use the teacher's vocabulary as a mask that hides their lack of conceptual understanding? Does the teacher encourage students to talk, argue, and construct their own understandings?

During each day of our involvement, the classroom was alive with student movement and noise; it seemed to be an ideal learning environment. Early in the year, students were working in groups of four, tracking hurricanes across weather maps, designing continents with appropriate topological features, and experimenting with air pressure effects. The teacher and a student teacher moved around the room and talked with them.

We noticed that the experienced teacher had taken on several tasks: He organized his classroom into work areas with displays that encouraged free movement and talk, he instructed directly when he opened each class with a mini-lesson on the day's topic, then gave students approximately thirty-five minutes to work in four-member teams on the day's assignment. He also translated scientific concepts by using non-science-specific vocabulary. The teacher's instructional strategies included a curious dichotomy. On one hand, he used nontraditional methods, notably collaborative learning. On the other hand, he seemed reluctant to step away from the center of the students' attention, wary of truly giving students the responsibility for learning what he sets in motion.

This teacher regularly used the traditional triadic dialogue pattern of teacher question, student answer, and teacher confirmation (or evaluation) described by Lemke in *Talking Science: Language, Learning, and Values* (Lemke 1990, 9). For example, during a discussion following an examination he asked a student to explain her answer describing how meteorologists track hurricanes. She replied, "I put that they use air pressure and temperature, but you marked it wrong." He responded, "No, remember when we practiced using latitude and longitude on the hurricane maps? That's what I was looking for." Instead of creating a learning situation that might help students question *how* they arrived at their answers, he offered his explanation for passive reception. The posttest review session, a terrific idea, fell short of its potential because of the traditional teacher-as-authority tone.

We noticed, too, that students were rarely asked to read information from a textbook or to make sense of information from other authoritative sources. Seldom did this teacher make explicit the connections between scientific terms and his more familiar yet non-science-specific vocabulary. He seemed to assume that students would readily understand scientific concepts when familiar language was used. We were interested in checking the validity of this assumption, because it seemed that learning to use a familiar word in a new, unfamiliar context can be as difficult as learning a new word when in association with a new concept. During a lesson on hurricanes, we heard the teacher open the discussion by saying that "storms appear" and close it with "storms disappear." Even though students and teacher used words such as "longitude," "latitude," and "prime meridian" during the lesson, the words "appear" and "disappear" were regularly substituted for science-specific explanations of how storms form and dissipate. We considered the question, "What effect does this teacher's use of 'storms appear' and 'storms disappear' have on students' understanding of the formation and dissipation of storms?" It seemed to us that by using these non-science-specific terms, words that verge on a magical or mystical explanation of storms, the teacher effectively shut down further inquiry from students. We agree with Wolfe and Maguire, who explain in chapter 3 that students' use of familiar language may facilitate their initial formation of personal concepts. However, we are concerned with students' use of familiar language as a vehicle for disguising failure to understand, and with the teacher's false assumption that students who can reiterate or even paraphrase his familiar words necessarily have constructed personal understanding. In our example, the students were already familiar with "appear" and "disappear" and agreed with the teacher on the general meaning of his words; therefore, there was no need for further negotiation and thus real construction of meaning—learning—did not occur.

The influence of non-science-specific vocabulary on construction of meaning is evident in a student's description of typhoons, hurricanes, and storms: "I learned that storms that form in the Pacific Ocean are called typhoons, and hurricanes start as tropical storms and then they turn into hurricanes and they always start in the Atlantic Ocean off the coast of Africa. Then they move forward Northeast and then when they get further up North they die down." This journal entry suggests the student's lack of conceptualization of storms as science phenomena. It also raises a question of whether or not his level of understanding has been affected and possibly restricted by the teacher's metaphors "appear" and "disappear." It is interesting to note that the student translated the teacher's "disappear" as "die down." Implicit in the student's entry is a distorted understanding of science, shared between the teacher and student, that is grounded in a notion of a magical force instead of the scientific principles involved in storm formation. Lemke refers to this kind of perception as an example of the perpetuation of the "certain harmful mystique of science" (1990, ix).

An example of a student's attempt to use scientific discourse in order to disguise her lack of understanding of a concept emerged when she explained that the purpose for learning how to graph the results of a probabilities experiment was to "help us learn to *observate*." Not only did her response end with a pseudoscientific mispronunciation, but more important, the response indicates that she misunderstood the relationship of the graph to the experiment. She thought that watching the experiment helped her draw a graph, but she did not realize that the graph could help her make sense of the results of the experiment, and thus construct knowledge about what she observed.

Lemke suggests that the root of such misunderstandings may be a teacher's failure to explain "the specific relationships of scientific meanings to one another, and how those relationships are assembled into thematic patterns" (1990, 21). He asserts that the *patterns* of meaning used to present information, including lectures, discussions, group talk, textbooks, lab notes, and research reports, are rarely explained to students as forms of academic discourse. It is likely that teachers of middle school science erroneously assume that, even before students learn science, they can read and speak science in discourse forms practiced by scientists.

Evidence of the need to explain patterns or forms of science discourse is provided in a seventh grader's journal entry. She was asked, "What have you learned this week about weather elements?" She replied: "We really haven't learned anything yet because we are experimenting and also doing projects." The project to which she referred involved collecting information about an assigned weather topic in the library—with no direct supervision—and presenting an oral report of her findings. Her initial entry indicates that she did not understand a connection between process and information. However, an entry she wrote two weeks later indicated that she has learned, with experience, that she must actively negotiate and construct meaning in order to make sense of scientific phenomena:

> Today in our group we talked about how tornadoes start off white but when they hit the ground they turn gray. I said that was really surprising to me. I guess I never thought about the colors of tornadoes before.

In addition to his roles as organizer, instructor, and translator, we also observed the teacher filling some roles of a scientist. He set up, conducted, and interpreted the results of experiments. Students were then asked to use class time to replicate his experiments. Out of class they were to conduct their own experiments, researching questions such as garbage output patterns and recycling benefits in their own households. When outside experiments were completed, the teacher explained how to interpret the findings. Again, the notion of a single correct interpretation of data was promoted by the teacher; student thinking was not.

What can we learn from one teacher's middle school science classes? For one thing, we see that the language used by a teacher matters: It may interfere with students' understanding of science concepts. We wonder how often students pick up on a teacher's vocabulary and duplicate it in order to play a game of hiding their lack of understanding with appropriate diction.

Following is an example of how the teacher's vocabulary can obfuscate student learning. Before asking students to plot the movement of a tropical storm, the teacher announced, "I'm going to give you the coordinates and you'll put the tropical storm there." He then asked, "Who knows what the coordinate system is?" When only one student raised her hand, he followed the first question by asking, "Who has ever played Battleship?" Several hands went up; the teacher replied, "See, you do know the coordinate system. You use it to move up and down and across." The brief reference to the game Battleship was never developed. The direct comparison of the way the game uses the coordinate system and the way tropical storms are tracked is a connection that the teacher assumed his students were able to make. He found later that they needed more help in understanding the comparison.

An example of how middle school students mimic their teacher's vocabulary to confirm data regardless of whether or not they understand scientific concepts emerged as students worked in groups tracking a storm on weather maps. Students typically asked: "Is this location correct?" and "Does this look like it's supposed to?" A more thoughtful question might have been: "How can a storm move from one location to another?" Neither the students nor the teacher showed deep concern for learning the underlying principles of science. Once an answer was approved, there was no further consideration of what the dot meant in terms of longitude and latitude, or even how the coordinate system had been used. With correct answers (or correct language) at their fingertips, students saw no reason to make sense of the activity for themselves. The activity fell short of leading students to use their own experiences and observations in order to construct meaning—to learn.

Students knew how to use language and activity to play the school game. The behavior and language of the students was directed toward showing the teacher they were on task; a glance around the room would show the observer students bent over their maps, sharing with each other and in deep discussion. They were playing the game of school like experts. However, even though students appeared to be working on the academic task, most conversations were directed primarily toward getting a right answer. One student would look at another's map and let him or her know that the marks needed to be repositioned. Group discussions tended to be social or procedural, not academic.

Science seemed to be treated as either inexplicable magic or as a body of facts that can be understood simply through knowledge of key vocabulary. Much procedural information was processed by students, but there was little evidence that equal amounts of construction of scientific concepts was developing. Note the context of this journal entry:

> Today, I learned an enormous amount of knowledge. Like when clouds go very high they evaporate or turn to rain. And in order to get a higher grade go deeper in thought and be specific with your imagination of words.

This student offered his teacher and us more insight into his learning (or lack thereof) than he realized. Has this student reduced the study of science to a set of facts to be memorized, a list of his teacher's classroom management expectations? For him, does science even exist outside of the science classroom? Does his teacher attend to such telling remarks? The teacher diligently responded to journal entries, adding comments such as "But how did the storm move from Mexico to Florida?" and "This sounds more like a thoughtful entry than the ones you wrote last week!" Yet he seemed hesitant to allow students to use language—to talk science—in an exploratory way. Students' efforts to synthesize and evaluate information went, for the most part, unrewarded. Why? Possibly because such responses were not typical or not anticipated by the teacher. In this classroom, lessons that were ostensibly science lessons were often devoid of concern for the learning of science. Our findings support Lemke's assertion:

> Students are not taught *how* to *talk* science: how to put together workable science sentences and paragraphs, how to combine terms and meanings, how to speak, argue, analyze, or write science. . . . When they don't catch on, we conclude that they weren't bright enough or didn't try hard enough. But we don't directly teach them how to. . . . Is it any wonder that very few succeed? Or that those from social backgrounds where the activity structures, preferred grammar, rhetorical patterns, and

> figures of speech that they are used to are least like those of
> science and the classroom do least well? (1990, 22)

Teachers of science must consider how often learning to construct scientific understanding is obstructed by our classroom practices.

Is it possible that middle school English/language arts teachers can learn from the conversations and conventions of their colleagues' science classes? And is it possible that the English/language arts teacher may be able to contribute to middle school students' understanding of science? We believe the answer to these questions is yes. Current middle school philosophy and practice are based in large part on the premise that interdisciplinary studies benefit teachers and students. We believe, too, that the problem of teaching students "how to talk science" (Lemke 1990, 22) can provide an impetus for science and English/language arts teachers to work purposefully in truly collaborative teams.

How might science and language arts teachers work together to help students think and learn? We saw students who did not understand the specialized ways in which the teacher used several common words during lectures, demonstrations, and direction giving. Collaborative planning and teaching between science and language arts teachers could contribute greatly to students' learning of critical reading and listening skills. Comprehension monitoring and other metacognitive practices could also be taught and reinforced by both teachers; such practices would demonstrate to students that critical thinking skills ignore traditional subject area boundaries.

We saw students sent to the library to research report topics; they went straight to the encyclopedias and copied passages, never slowing to monitor their comprehension or to make sense of the textual information. Their subsequent oral reports were uninspired and uninspiring. One student, unable to decipher her research partner's handwriting chose to delete words such as "air," "wind," "barometer," and "pressure," words that were essential for a listener who hoped to make sense of the presentation. The partner congratulated her on a "great job." If the research assignment is to be a valuable learning experience, the language arts teacher could teach, during her class, the skills of reading, reviewing, and recording information from a variety of reference sources. She probably already does, but perhaps her work would be more effective if linked to a meaningful science research assignment.

We also saw (and applauded) the science teacher assigning a

response journal in order to encourage his students to reflect on and organize what they were learning. In evaluating the effectiveness of his journal assignments, the teacher concluded that with more direct instruction, he could help students learn to use journals as a place where questions can emerge in order to fuel problem solving.

Our study provides convincing evidence that language must be treated as an active force that is at work in all classes. Primarily, our work demonstrates the need for teachers to attend carefully to student-student and student-teacher discourse. It also implies that all teachers need to consider their roles as rhetors: Perhaps serious self-examination will reveal that we spend too much time talking and too little time listening to our students. We must explore the real benefits of small and whole group discussion as a means of allowing students to construct meaning; to do so will mean that we resist the temptation to promote convergent thinking and to reward only those students who are able to reiterate our finite set of facts. If we fail to listen to students' authentic questions and insights, we give them the signal that their ideas are unimportant. Conversely, by listening intently, we indicate that we believe they are capable of constructing meaning. Such meaning then becomes personally-significant learning.

References

Harris, R. A. 1991. Rhetoric of Science. *College English*, 53: 282–307.

Lemke, J. 1990. *Talking Science: Language Learning and Values.* Norwood, N.J.: Ablex.

7 Science and Society: Escape to the Real World

Betty Carvellas, Brad Blanchette, and Lauren Parren
Colchester High School, Colchester, Vermont

One morning our librarian rushed into our classroom waving a photograph from *The Burlington Free Press*. It featured Sean Beaver, a Science and Society student, in front of a McDonald's, brandishing a sign protesting the use of styrofoam for fast food packaging. In our course it is not enough for students merely to research topics, create annotated bibliographies, form opinions, write position papers, and disseminate conclusions to their peers; they must also *take action* based on their findings and their convictions. Sean had become one of our more impassioned and effective environmentalists—not what many would have expected from a student who, for most of his schooling, had been classified as a student with special needs. This was no surprise to us, however, because Sean chose his own topic, conducted thorough research, and believed in what he was trying to accomplish. Confronted with real-world issues that potentially affect their lives, students invariably translate personal interest into hard work. (Our McDonald's discontinued the use of styrofoam shortly after the protest).

High school students are growing up in a society where technological advances occur at an increasing rate. Today's factual knowledge may well be obsolete by the time these students graduate. Nevertheless, many textbooks, particularly in the sciences, exhibit a growing tendency to become even more fact-filled and vocabulary-laden. It is not uncommon in high school courses for students to memorize information, pass tests, and complete a course with little real comprehension of underlying principles. Future citizens will have a difficult time making informed decisions based on this kind of learning. Realizing that students need to develop critical thinking skills in order to be technologically literate, we designed Science and Society, a team-taught course that stresses research, talking, writing, and thinking.

Science and Society is not a typical high school course. The teachers do not lecture; there is no textbook; the students do not take

objective unit tests. Recognizing that high school students will soon
be responsible for making decisions in an increasingly technological
society, we hope Science and Society helps students to:

1. Become skillful at obtaining factual information from a variety
   of sources reflecting multiple points of view. (Students produce annotated bibliographies.)

2. Process information and make informed decisions based on
   their findings. (Students produce position papers after they
   learn to recognize bias, distinguish fact from opinion, and
   use statistics.)

3. Act on their beliefs. (Students write letters to their elected
   representatives and to newspapers, hold debates for the
   public, and produce slide shows, among other things.)

4. Formulate personal philosophies that are applied consistently
   across issues. (Students develop personal statements of belief
   as part of their take-home examination.)

Although students eventually select the topics we study, we
begin the year by assigning articles on Science, Technology, and Society
(STS) topics to teams of students who present summaries and critical
reviews to the class. Following the presentations, students individually
brainstorm a potential list of additional STS topics. Inevitably their
lists include topics such as euthanasia, biotechnology, animal rights,
acid rain, toxic waste, energy, science and the military, feeding the
hungry, and artificial intelligence. Teachers participate in brainstorming,
adding topics students may have been unaware of or simply forgot.
After we synthesize their ideas into one comprehensive list, students
rank their top five choices, and we compile the subjects for the year.

At the start of each individual unit of study is a five-minute
freewrite. Students are told to write continually about the topic, not
being particularly concerned about spelling, punctuation, and usage.
This type of journal entry indicates the depth of existing knowledge
on the topic. As the students say, "It's a brain dump." After several
volunteers read their freewrites aloud, students jot down questions
that they have generated from the discussion. After listing the questions
on the blackboard, students use the list to select a specific controversial
topic for research; therefore, each student becomes responsible for one
aspect of the general subject. For example, during a recent unit about
biomedical issues, Geoffrey and Sally became interested in Christian
Science. After an initial investigation, they focused their inquiry on
Christian Science parents' rights, i.e., restricting medical attention for
seriously ill minors. During the same unit, Ruby and Willy analyzed

contemporary attitudes in the United States and juxtaposed them with the liberal government-supported euthanasia policies in the Netherlands.

Once students choose individual topics, much of the class time is spent in the library, where students learn to use selectively a wide variety of resources. At the beginning of the year, students may turn to *The Readers' Guide to Periodical Literature* (annotated version on CD-ROM). Following a workshop given by the librarian, they are more apt to select sources such as *Newsbank* and *Christian Science Monitor* on CD-ROM, *Facts on File, SIRS,* federal directories (*Washington Information Directory, Federal Regulatory Directory*), *Historic Documents,* and vertical files both in the classroom and in the library.

As the school year progresses, students become adept at using the phone to seek information from local, state, and national agencies. They quickly recognize the need for background reading before contacting busy professionals. Interviewing skills are perfected to the point where students reach for the phone as often as they delve into more traditional sources. It was an exciting moment for Shane when he dialed Citizen's Clearinghouse for Hazardous Waste in Washington in pursuit of information and realized he was speaking to Lois Gibbs, a Love Canal community activist who founded the Clearinghouse! Similarly, Ed could not believe his luck when Derek Humpfry, director of the Hemlock Society, granted him a telephone interview as part of his research. Connecting with experts in the real world—many of whom they have read about—energizes not only the individual conducting the interview but all the students, who realize that these experts regard them as knowledgeable persons.

Like most students, the young people in our course initially accept as fact whatever they see in print or hear from authorities. Over the course of the year, students learn to anticipate bias in sources and actively seek opposing points of view. They become critical consumers of information. At the conclusion of their research, students write an annotated bibliography, reflecting balanced and thorough research.

It is very difficult at first for students accustomed to "right" answers to form an opinion after having examined all sides of an issue. Students often tell us that this is the most challenging portion of the course. Kris, Angel, and Maria struggled with their own positions after researching the issue of whether voters should allow Burlington, Vermont, to buy power from Hydro-Quebec. They invited two guest speakers to visit the class: the mayor of Burlington and a representative from Burlington Electric. Each represented an opposing perspective and provided us with abundant data, but the information served to make the student researchers' decision even more difficult. After all, here were two authorities whom they had grown up watching on the local news, both sincere, both knowledgeable, but each contradicting the other. This confusion forced Kris, Angel, and Maria to review their previous findings to determine where to go next. After more library research, they decided that difficult problems are best clarified by a risk management process that helps them identify issues, separate fact from opinion, propose solutions, and predict consequences of various solutions.

Oral presentations and class discussion help students clarify their positions while allowing teachers to evaluate student progress. Students are assessed according to their ability to explain and defend a position in an oral presentation followed by a question-and-answer period. It takes time to develop an attitude where young people question the logic of a position without attacking the individual presenter. Students soon recognize that the questions are designed to help the presenter solidify his or her position. After students have defended their positions to their peers and to us, they write meticulously documented position papers using the guidelines of the Modern Language Association.

Perhaps what makes Science and Society unique is the action project. Since one of our primary goals is to teach students to become responsible citizens, we emphasize that forming an opinion is not sufficient; the next step is to take action to effect change. Initially, the students believe that their opinions do not matter. A typical comment is, "Why should anyone care what I think?" The first published letter to the editor or response from an elected official changes that attitude. Typical action projects include letters to newspaper and magazine editors, legislators, enforcement agencies, and corporate executives. In addition, students have testified before a legislative committee, presented a debate on public radio, set up information booths in local shopping centers, walked a picket line, and coordinated community presentations.

U.S. Senator Patrick Leahy has visited our class, and students were thrilled to find their comments and picture in his newsletter to constituents:

> What does the average Vermont high school student know about
> what goes on in Washington? Plenty—if my recent visit

to . . . Colchester High School is any indication of the interest and knowledge our young people have in the workings and performance of the federal government. Students asked me questions on acid rain, arms control, apartheid, defense spending, Nicaragua, dairy price supports, famine in Ethiopia, the drinking age, state government, and the trappings of power in Washington.

Students often invite professionals such as lawyers, doctors, professors, and legislators to speak to the class. A frequent guest in our class, for example, is the founder of the Vermonters Organized for Cleanup (VOC), a grassroots program that addresses the issue of toxic waste. One dynamic and controversial pair of speakers was a fundamentalist, antiabortion rights minister and a director of Planned Parenthood of Vermont, who asked not to be in the same room together. Their presentations allowed the students the opportunity to observe how people can take the same set of facts and draw totally different conclusions.

Some students organize field trips, such as the one we took to view acid rain damage on Camel's Hump Mountain. Others respond creatively, through projects such as silk-screened T-shirts, sculptures, paintings, and songs. Karrie and Michael wrote a play about acid rain, featuring King Evil Cloud, Sad Spruce, Rotten Raindrop, and Super Citizen. Fifth graders performed the play (complete with costumes, teacher's guide, and a coloring book for each student) in elementary schools throughout the district. Students reach out to the community through their action projects. They coordinate evening panel discussions, produce and distribute fliers, present at state-wide conferences, and testify before state legislative committees. A few years ago, the entire class organized a day-long STS symposium, involving many professionals from the community and reaching a large percentage of the student body.

While the previously discussed format fills a major portion of class time, other strategies supplement the general curriculum. Two weekly journal assignments and a weekly log fulfill three goals: holding students accountable for daily progress, catalyzing reflection of personal learning, and keeping students abreast of current events. Simulation games, value-clarification activities, field trips, and role-play activities provide a break from the usual routine. Drawing on ideas from *Creative Role Playing Exercises in Science and Technology* (developed by the Social Science Education Consortium of Boulder, Colorado), our students conducted a mock FDA hearing on the AIDS drug-approval process. Each student assumed a new identity: some served as constituent representatives on the FDA panel; others testified as members of various advocacy groups. We heard from the mother of a gay man with AIDS, intravenous drug users, liberal and conservative clergy, health care workers, public health officials. The hearing was held in the library complete with lights, microphones, and video cameras.

The goal of helping students formulate philosophies that are consistent with their personal values is addressed by a final examination that encourages a new kind of thinking for most of our students. This take-home exam asks them to review their position papers for each of the issues we have studied. Sometimes students take what appear to be inconsistent stands, and we encourage them to analyze the incongruities. We hope this analysis will give them a base from which to operate when confronted with new issues. While there is no one correct answer, we do look for insightful analysis of the variety of positions taken throughout the year. For example, if students are *for* abortion and *opposed* to euthanasia, we want them to examine what they mean by the value of life. Where do they draw the line? In what circumstances might they change their minds?

Team teaching is rewarding for students and teachers. Students learn to break down some of the artificial barriers dividing learning in most school settings. Teachers learn from each other and grow intellectually and professionally. It requires the right blend of personalities to teach together; flexibility and self-confidence need to be equally balanced. Teachers need to be competent in their own fields and believe that both students and teachers benefit from exploring an area of inquiry together. They need to share big goals as well as details like grading, due dates, class rules, and the myriad of other factors involved in running a class. Although team teaching is one ideal, we recognize that it is not always feasible. The primary goals of the class—to develop technological literacy, citizen responsibility, and language proficiency—are adaptable to science, social studies, and English courses.

We have heard from several former students who tell us that Science and Society has had a positive impact on their lives. It has helped some to be more successful in college, and it has helped others to be more politically involved. Students consistently tell us in their journals that Science and Society makes them think and prepares them for what they perceive to be the real world. Parents have told us that our class is a constant source of dinner conversation. Visiting teachers from across the state have expressed surprise at the quality of work produced by our students. We love teaching this course because it works. Students walk in the door discussing the issues and stay after the bell. As Susie wrote, "It isn't the type of class where you fall asleep listening to the teacher lecture. Yes, this class is a lot of work and is challenging, but that's what helps make it fun. I like learning about things that are going to have an impact on my life. This class is the best—the perfect way to end the day."

Resources

There are no assigned texts for Science and Society. Three useful supplementary sources are:

Butterfield, C. 1983. *Values and Biology.* Portland, Maine: J. Weston Walsh.

Newton, D. 1983. *Science and Social Issues.* Portland, Maine: J. Weston Walsh.

Parisi, L., ed. 1986. *Creative Role Playing Exercises in Science and Technology.* Boulder, Colo.: Social Science Education Consortium, Inc.

Another valuable resource is the series of books entitled *Taking Sides,* published by The Dushkin Publishing Co.

8 Bridging the Gap between *The Two Cultures*

Erica Jacobs
Thomas Jefferson High School of Science and Technology,
Alexandria, Virginia

... a dandelion by
Taraxacum officinale
Smells just like bright and summer and warm and yellow
Doesn't it?
And maybe a
Taraxacum officinale
is just a feeling of
bright and summer and warm and yellow and
Meaningful.
To someone who wonders.

                                        Eric Scheirer

In 1959, when C. P. Snow lamented the rift between the sciences and humanities in *The Two Cultures,* he could not have had today's high school student in mind. But as U.S. students fall behind their counterparts abroad in math and science skills, schools are increasingly emphasizing science, technology, and related subjects. How do those of us who teach nontechnical areas bridge the gap between "the two cultures?"

I have asked myself this question many times in the four years I have been an English teacher in Virginia's seven-year-old Thomas Jefferson High School for Science and Technology. Our English, social studies, and foreign language departments have all been struggling for identities; the students and the parents frequently question the importance of these "soft" subjects in a technical school. We also are teased by colleagues in neighboring "regular" schools who inquire, "Do your techies write in English, or in computerese?"

But every time I've asked myself about the gap, the answer has remained the same, a consistency that still surprises me: We need no special skill to bridge the gap between "the two cultures" because the gap is an artificial one of our own making. Literary critics, writers, and historians look carefully at the world, its inhabitants, and their creations; scientists do the same thing. We are bound by a single objective: to find pattern and meaning in the world as we see it. This is not news to Lewis Thomas or Stephen Jay Gould, even if it does seem to be news to teachers of nontechnical disciplines.

Thomas Jefferson High School encourages cross-disciplinary teaching, although our moves in that direction have been gradual. All tenth- and eleventh-grade English and social studies classes are combined and team taught as "humanities" courses. Our most innovative integrated course is the required ninth-grade triple block, in which groups of seventy-five students meet their biology, English, and technology teachers in three successive periods. The block can combine into one seventy-five student class for various projects. When the students write up findings from a technology lab, or report on land use for a biology field trip, their English teacher is part of the revising and grading process. They read scientific articles for all three teachers, and they may write a technothriller fantasy in tech language or English. Each team shares the philosophy that observing life, writing about life, and improving our lives are connected disciplines.

This vision of connection is part of the school's publications, sponsored by teachers of science and technology as well as English. In *Teknos,* our journal of science, mathematics, and technology, Todd Dampier contributes "An Efficient Lagrangian Molecular Dynamics Model in a Massively Parallel Computing Environment"; in *Threshold,* the less technical arts and sciences magazine, Todd writes "The Last Picture Show," a lyrical essay about the Voyager 2 spacecraft. The titles alone are lessons in how divergent the forms of scientific writing can be. *Threshold* publishes creative computer programs as well as our more traditional examples of creative writing. Each publication tries to mirror the students' experience at Jefferson—an experience that, at its best, gives students the technical tools and scientific techniques to observe and draw conclusions, and the literary tools and techniques to write about their findings with clarity and grace.

I first noticed the scientific method transposed into my subject in literary criticism. I always remind my students that the word "analysis" means the same thing in English as it does in science or mathematics—the breaking down of a subject into its component parts. After all, isn't literary analysis similar to analytic geometry? or analytic chemistry? I am never sure my analogies work until the first piece of criticism comes in. Andrew, a student who has never felt unusually proficient in English, follows his accustomed method as he analyzes the book *Dubliners* by James Joyce. First he notes some characteristics exhibited in the fourteen short stories:

> Everything in this book is twisted . . . Everyone and everything is off-kilter, abnormal. Joyce has included every type of perversion possible, spanning the range from alcoholism ("The Dead," "Counterparts," "Araby," "A Painful Case"), to pederasty, implied and real ("The Sisters" and "An Encounter" respectively), to overbearing mothers ("The Boarding House," "A Mother"), and fathers ("Eveline," "Counterparts").

At this point Andrew, a good observer, finds the common denominator:

> Though these perversions always seem to appear in multiple stories, no thread is carried all the way through, not even alcoholism—no thread, that is, except . . . the sickness of distorted love. There is only one instance of love gone right in the entire book. In every other case, love either goes wrong or is wrong, or at least slightly bent.

Having found the theme that links all fourteen stories, Andrew proceeds, in analytical fashion, to explicate the instances of distorted love. At the end Andrew, who has become a literary critic by virtue of his observations, reveals a greater message.

> The end . . . is where the sicknesses and perversions of love are all set aright. Gabriel is a very plain person; what defines him is his concept of love . . . Though his concept of love is shaken up at the end, it emerges, stronger than before. The message seems to be that love is something that has been lost to the citizens of Dublin, though they attempt in vain to achieve it. Only one man could set it right. Maybe we're supposed to be like him; the point is that love can come out okay, once in a blue moon perhaps, but it can happen . . . I'd really rather be like him, and love like him, than like any other character in the book.

Andrew concludes, like many essays of literary criticism, with an echo of James Joyce's own declaration of intention: "I guess *Dubliners* is a moral fable, after all."

As Andrew has figured out intuitively, the process of classifying in literature is similar to the construction of a typology of scientific data: You examine particular characteristics; note any common denominators; then categorize the sample set in terms of their similarities. The scientist, as well as the literary critic, must ask at the end: "Does this apply to me?" "What difference does this observation make on the way I view the world?"

Creative writing as well as literary criticism makes use of the talents of these young scientists. Sianne's poem on playground memories observes the world in terms of concrete images:

> ... The basket hoops were rusted and made of
>   steel chains; to match the fence I guess
> So we played one-on-one and five-on-five
>   and twenty-one and horse and pig and piggy
> and sometimes aardvark (ha-ha, Curtis)
>   shirts-and-skins, darks-and-lights, tans-and-burns
> We ate Choco-Chips from the ice cream truck
>   harassed little kids
>   and talked long and loud about
> who would make it to the playoffs, the score of the game
>   and which teacher was ugliest and why.
>
> But nights
>   sometimes we would sneak out the window
> and meet on the courts (which were somehow kind of different)
>   and we would talk
> about things like war, and love, and hate, and the things
> that could have never been said, and would never have been
>   heard
>   over the sounds of the rusty nets squeaking, and
>   the slapping of bare feet on hot blacktop.
> All of us
>   Chris and Paul and Eric and Derek and Andy
>   proud me the only girl and Curtis of course
> sprawled on the melting lines of the basketball courts.

Precisely what makes this visually rich (the "rusted hoops," "which teacher was ugliest," "Bare feet on hot blacktop," "melting lines") also makes this an accurate reproduction of Sianne's experience. The method of looking at events, enumerating them in detail, then deriving their significance can be employed by the essayist as well as the poet. It is also the scientific method we know as induction.

Each spring I ask my seniors to write a "good-bye" poem, letter, or essay that we compile into a class book. Responses range from love letters to odes on a locker. Often their technical backgrounds find a place in these farewell pieces. Quang sees the neutron as a metaphor for the process of separation:

> Neutron
> A well-grooved orbit
> about a nucleus
> and yet straining
> fighting the forces

of nature;
a
    Break-away,
        a sudden, violent thrust of energy away from the
    mass disappearing;
alone in
Oblivion.

Even a simple narration becomes more evocative when it recreates the outside world in the author's terms. Alessandra's college-application essay records the events of a rainy day in which she wandered around Washington and ended up in the botanical garden:

> It was filled with the strangest, most interesting plants, from cacti to ferns. We found a spot we liked and sat down to rest. It was a little bridge over a stream with two big palm trees on the sides, and surrounded by colorful flowers. At either end there were some large amphoras with exotic-looking paintings on them. I felt like I was in ancient Babylonia.

The attention to detail that makes this a good application essay also shows a bit of the botanist peeking through. Those identities are complementary, not mutually exclusive.

Reinforcing this point is Sianne's senior project in the biotechnology lab. Just as her poetry exhibited the scientific method, her lab reports exhibit literary devices. As she compares the drip loss from frozen sections of banana and celery cells, she observes that banana cells,

> clingy and rounded in shape, and tightly packed to one another in a dense network, had thick, strong-looking cell membranes closely aligned with the cell walls, trapping a thin layer of air tightly in between to provide an extra 'layer' of reinforcement. Squarish, rectangular celery cells, however, were very loosely placed together, like old bricks stacked in a wall. Most importantly, however, they had very thin, porous, weak-looking cell membranes that were detached, separated, and floating disjointedly around within the cell wall. This led to the theory that the thickness and durability of a cell membrane are significant influences on a plant or animal cell's chances of nutritional or structural retention after freezing.

The non-science-oriented reader can see the two sorts of cells juxtaposed: the banana "clingy" and "tightly packed," alongside the celery, "like old bricks stacked in a wall" with membranes that float "disjointedly." The simile and vivid adverbial phrases allow us to see why freezing alters the texture of celery, but doesn't ruin the texture of a banana.

Like Quang, Julie (who lives on a farm) finds it natural to observe events as a metaphor through which we can come closer to an understanding of the world, in this case, the birth of a goat:

> Kids come out pretty much the same way children do: bloody and wet. And always in the middle of winter, on the coldest night. . . . My father usually goes down to the barn every few hours when we are expecting. When he finds a newborn, he brings it in and our house smells like a goat factory for a few weeks; it's a small price to pay. Usually this works, only my father wasn't there the night Juliette gave birth . . .
>
> All through the night, through the ordeal of running to the house for a towel and running back, then running to the house again with a wet, shivering kid, I never once thought of all the other animals who had been born and died before this one ever came along. All I could think of while I was milking Juliette with stiff, cold hands was how much I loved that little ugly thing. And it was ugly, bow-legged, and top heavy from a head two sizes too big. I loved it anyway.
>
> I had never really thought about life or death before. It was just something that happened and I had never questioned it; I had never had to. Lying in bed that night, I began to wonder what right that baby downstairs had to live when other animals died . . .

As with Sianne's poem and Alessandra's essay, what makes Julie's narrative good is not just what she sees, but what she concludes from what she sees. All three have looked at ordinary natural phenomena, and discovered a meaning, even a truth. There is something rather remarkable in the process of examining the world's physical properties: You can learn why bananas freeze better than celery; you can recreate the lush exoticism of ancient Babylonia in a modern botanical garden; you might even learn something about love and hate on a playground, or about life and death in a barn at midnight. There is something wondrous about looking at the world closely; and that is not exclusive to writers, or poets, or scientists. It is something we all share.

This sense of wonder is perhaps best illustrated in a poem by Eric, one of the school's most distinguished computer and science students:

> The mind of a scientist
> Has been said to remove mystery
> meaning Wonder

From the world.
And yes, a scientist can see a
dandelion and
Declare
it to be not bright and summer and warm and yellow
but
Taraxacum officinale.

But the words of the
Learn'd Astronomer
who has become as famous as a poem
can send us
Outside to discover our own world with
Its own stars.
Maybe its own mystery.

And anyway, a dandelion by
Taraxacum officinale
Smells just like bright and summer and warm and yellow
Doesn't it?
And maybe a
Taraxacum officinale
is just a feeling of
bright and summer and warm and yellow and
Meaningful.
To someone who wonders.

"Wonder" is at the heart of the scientific method, but it is also at the heart of literature and all writing. The ability to look carefully at the world and ask "why?" allows these "techies" a perspective that makes their creative writing as revealing as their lab reports. There is no trick to bridging the gap between the two cultures—beyond realizing that the gap need not exist.

Reference

Snow, C. P. 1964. *The Two Cultures: And a Second Look.* 2d ed. Cambridge University Press.

9 From Tourist to Storyteller: Reading and Writing Science

Dawn Abt-Perkins and Gian Pagnucci
University of Wisconsin–Madison

"Gian, you've got to hear this," said Dawn. "Listen to how Julius was reading the article."

Julius was sitting with his partner, Karla, analyzing his reading strategies from journal entries made while reading an article titled "Slavery in Ants" from *Scientific American*. All of the students in the class had been asked to read a scientific article and record in their journals their responses, comments, and questions of the texts while reading. Now they were working in pairs or small groups of three to describe each others' reading processes based on these journal entries. The goal of the assignment was to help them gain some insight into their own reading as well as learn new reading strategies.

Dawn had overheard Julius tell his partner that he had pretended the article was a story. When he did that, it became interesting and easy to read. He said he had made jokes with the author as if the author had been sitting in the same room telling a story about watching ants.

Karla said the article seemed pretty dry to her, not much like a story. But Julius said it had a beginning, middle, and end like other stories. It even seemed to him that it built to a suspenseful climax when it referred to the violence that occurred between the ants. He could picture himself telling this kind of a story because he had watched ants for nearly an hour a few days before in his animal behavior research class.

We were in the second week of a reading class that was part of a six-week Summer Science Institute (SSI) sponsored by the UW–Madison Graduate School, the Center for Biology Education, and Chicago State University. The purpose of the institute was to give students an opportunity to *be* scientists. They were expected to design and carry out a research project. The driving philosophy of the program argued that students learn science best by engaging in scientific inquiry. Students spent their mornings in reading, writing, and math classes to teach them the basics they needed in the afternoons, when they tackled their research with the help of working scientists. Different groups of students studied animal behavior, exercise physiology, genetics, and forensic chemistry.

The students were chosen for the program based on their strong interest in science and their nontraditional cultural, social, and economic backgrounds. Based only on grades and teacher recommendations, these students were considered average. But, in fact, they brought a variety of scientific interests and experiences to the program. These students came from a variety of different communities and social backgrounds. They represented African American, Latino, Chicano, and Southeast Asian cultures. Many were from low-income families. The students all shared an enthusiasm for science. The institute was designed to strengthen their commitment to science by giving them the opportunity to become contributing members of a scientific community.

When class was over, we talked about Julius and his use of a story to help him understand the complex scientific text we had assigned. In essence, Julius was doing what Jerome Bruner claims we all do when we communicate: Julius was grappling with difficult new material and textual structure by drawing on his more familiar, well-established narrative understanding. Bruner tells us that children, even in their earliest narratives, are integrating new information with their sense of how things are by creating stories (1990).

According to Bruner, we acquire and grow in our ability to communicate and understand our experience in language through applying narrative structures. He claims these include (1) means for emphasizing human action or understanding that there is an agent that drives experience; (2) sequential ordering of happenings; (3) sensitivity to the canonical in what is experienced; and (4) a narrator's perspective on an event (1990, 77). Julius used these same narrative principles to make sense of what he was reading to, in a way, converse with the text. Julius wanted to create a narrator to joke with, to believe that the author was someone who learned from watching ants the way that he himself had done. He saw the scientific text as having a plot, and he did not separate this type of reading experience from the kind he had with novels or short stories. By relating to the text as a story of a scientist at work, Julius's reading experience pointed out to us our students' need to humanize scientific reading and scientific action. Through connecting his experiences as a scientist with those of the text, Julius found a way to read himself into the story of science.

We decided to take a second look at the reading journals of the other students in the class. Many writings included references to story structures as students struggled to understand highly complex scientific texts from various disciplines. Like Julius, Ethel joked with the author. She responded to some of the difficult vocabulary in the text by writing, "These words are killing me." At other times she felt free to argue with the author's choice of words and descriptions. "You make them sound like stupid computers," she wrote when the author described the ants as "genetically programmed." At one point, she had an emotional reaction to one of the events described in the text: "If that happened to me, I would cry. I wonder if it could happen to people. I think the ants should distinguish their individualities." Ethel could see the narrator's perspective on the event and tried to create a conversation with the narrator to fully understand the text. Tonya, too, created a narrator with whom she conversed when she read a scientific report on the physiology of the koala. She asked, "How long has he been working and studying koalas?" And later, the conversation became more direct when she expressed frustration with the author's narrative style: "Going back and forth, back and forth. You are really getting on my nerves. I'm sure there is a better way."

While reading, our students were imagining the writer as the narrator of a scientific experience or scientific story. Two students, Kim and Brandon, found that Brandon even placed himself into the article about koalas as if he were a character in this story. Kim thought this made Brandon a reader who "lives the text." She believed this because Brandon's journal included emotional comments, such as "that would feel nice" when the author described a mother koala caring for its young.

While our students continued to read science articles as stories, we were teaching critical reading strategies such as summarizing main ideas, critiquing the quality of supporting evidence, recognizing rhetorical devices used to elevate credibility, and uncovering and analyzing the logical structure of the text. We continued to treat texts as artifacts of science, as constructed knowledge to be handed down to the reader. Meanwhile, our students resisted our framework and replaced reports of research processes with story plots, scientists with narrators, and scientific subjects with characters. They seemed interested in knowing the story of how the information came to be, not just the information itself. In fact, that was the primary way they made sense of it.

This became clear to us when the class read a scientific report titled "Drawing A Scientist Test: Future Implications." The paper was written by three women scientists who were interested in gender issues in science education. It reported on a study they conducted that involved asking high school students to draw pictures of scientists in order to isolate any stereotypic images of scientists the students might have had. Essentially, the report concluded that teachers could help scientific learning for young women by promoting a gender-free learning environment.

While we hoped our students would find the content interesting, we chose the reading primarily because it served as a model of the scientific reports that they needed to write for their research projects. Its format matched that of the traditional scientific report: *introduction, methods, results,* and *discussion.* Since this was the format the scientific community accepted, we intended to teach our students to communicate and understand scientific experiences in this way. As we read the article together, we hoped our students would begin to use the critical reading strategies we had suggested and demonstrated. But our instruction did not match what the students needed to successfully understand the article. For the students, story structures were still the best way to articulate their understanding of the text.

They understood the authors as fellow scientists trying to tell the story of what they had done. Some students observed that the researchers' first data analysis didn't show anything, so the scientists had done an alternative analysis to prove their hypothesis. Although this was not directly stated in the article, our students understood what the researchers had done because they had experienced a similar problem when working on a project in their genetics class. They also started to refer to the scientists who had written the article as "the authors who are telling the story" and continually referred to the "she" who had done the study when discussing the report. The young women in the class even tried to understand the motivation of the women scientists who had done the study: "I bet they wanted to study this because they weren't encouraged to study science when they were young girls like us." At the same time, some of the young men in the class lost interest in the article when they discovered that the scientists were women, and the problem they were studying was related to gender issues in science education. They felt left out, as if they couldn't relate to the conflict in the story. Our students needed to see the scientists at work behind the words in order to critique the presentation of information in the study. Somehow, our own idea of teaching critical strategic reading skills through a reading of this article became fruitless.

Because our students persisted in reading science in this personal, humanizing way, we thought they might want to know more about the lives of scientists and the ways scientists experienced their work. So, we supplemented the scientific reports and journal articles they were reading for their research with literature from the humanities: excerpts from *The John McPhee Reader,* Sue Hubbell's *A Country Year: Living the Questions,* and Aldo Leopold's *A Sand County Almanac.*

The students read these stories eagerly and wrote journal entries reflecting on how the writers described and commented on the acts of doing scientific inquiry. Tonya, a student of exercise physiology, admired how Hubbell worked as a keen observer of the natural environment that she lived in, always questioning and hypothesizing about the natural order of the world. Tonya saw the world through literary eyes, and that enriched her understanding of the meaning of her scientific work:

> I honestly and sincerely loved the way Sue Hubbell writes. She's very descriptive concerning her environment and all the animals living there. But yet she leaves room for one's imagination to perceive her in the environment. It's sort of like telling someone about something you did, but letting their imagination picture it. I like the method she uses. Because technically her story is a very descriptive, lengthy scientific observation report. But since no one gets really ecstatic about reading scientific jabba, she converts it to a calm, yet interesting story, that still gives the same amount of information and has a conclusion and an introduction. She just makes it more mysterious and exciting to read.

Alicia, who was studying animal behavior at the summer institute, saw parts of herself mirrored in the personality of Carol, one of the main characters in John McPhee's "Travels in Georgia." She wrote, "Carol's role was so intriguing. She was like a superwoman. She had no fear of anything in nature." In class discussions, Alicia related that she could see herself dissecting a pregnant turtle killed on the side of the road in order to preserve the eggs and stopping in the middle of a long car trip at the local library to find out exactly where a rare frog lived in the area, much as Carol had done in the story. Since Alicia had spent many afternoons in this summer program traipsing through woods to spend hours patiently listening and watching ducks and birds to learn how they communicate with each other, she could well understand that she too would be considered eccentric by some people's standards.

As our students roamed through these stories, finding themes, conflicts, and characters to understand and relate to, we discovered the literary dimensions of scientific understanding. But could we use this new knowledge to help our students fulfill the goals of the institute? Were our students learning to see themselves as scientists? Were they engaging in self-directed scientific inquiry?

The students had shown us that part of their transformation from student to scientist involved reading themselves into scientific roles and contexts. So we decided to have them write about their own scientific discoveries, the ones they were making in this program. They could use a standard scientific report, a story, or any other form of their choosing to tell each other about their discoveries. Although students had been writing scientific reports in their other classes and could have easily used one of them to fulfill the requirements of this assignment, all thirty-two students chose to write stories to communicate their discoveries to each other.

One student, Wan, wanted to write a story, but he was so concerned about writing such a nontraditional report that he checked several times to see if a story format was still acceptable. The students did not choose to write stories because they thought they were easy to write. Many students complained at first that they had made no scientific discoveries, that they didn't know how to tell a story, or that writing a story was just too hard. But as each student slowly articulated a story, that story's personal importance began to take control. The students wrote and rewrote, adding details or cutting points to give their stories life.

Bruner's work suggests that students depend on the "congenial and compelling medium" of stories when they are asked to reflect on their experiences:

> Children too have stories to tell and retell, not just from published materials but also from their own real and imagined worlds. In classrooms we can encourage them to take their own stances, to hypothesize about other worlds, other solutions to problems, whether these are social, literary, scientific or personal . . . As they become more reflective about—and critical of—their own stories, they also become more critical readers, writers, thinkers, and learners. (Bruner 1988, 574)

As our students wrote, they realized they needed outside opinions on how to improve their stories. They began to spontaneously exchange their stories. When a story was unclear or incomplete, the students insisted that the writer tell the rest of the story. Word of the best stories spread. Several students who hadn't worked very hard on the assignment decided to do rewrites after hearing about the good stories of others. By the time we got to discussing the stories formally in class, everyone wanted to read. "We want to hear stories," said Mitchell when his class was given a choice of what to do on a particular class day. And when we couldn't get through all of the stories in one class period, it was the students who pointed out whose stories were left to be read.

In the discovery stories our students told, Bruner's ideas about the learning power of stories held true. By communicating scientific experiences, our students established themselves in the role of author and agent of the inquiry. Through writing and telling the stories, many of the students began to articulate the questions they later pursued in their formal scientific research projects.

Brandon's "The Never Making Sense Story" was one example of the learning potential of storytelling. Brandon's story was about a time earlier in the program when he was the subject in an exercise physiology experiment. Because the students had written a report about this project, Brandon tried to use this report format to communicate his discovery to students in the other research areas. But after a couple of drafts, he realized that he couldn't explain his discovery adequately using the report format. He said he did not think other people would understand the report and that sometimes it was even confusing to him. In fact, Brandon had to work so hard to make sense of the experiment that this issue eventually found its way into his title.

The way Brandon finally made sense of his discovery was by turning his report about it into a story. He fictionalized himself and the class:

> "Okay men, any volunteers?" asked the captain. After a few seconds, a young man by the name of Daring Devon stepped forward. He had obviously taken so long to volunteer because he wanted to see who had the guts in his group.
> "You know men, this test calls for sure guts and stamina. You may get a huge headache that feels like a nuclear bomb. You will sweat, and you may become drowsy."
> Daring Devon sat in a hard blue chair with four legs. Facing

him was a huge blue cylinder full of oxygen and attached to the cylinder was a huge, hollow pipe with a blue mouth piece attached to it. He put his mouth around the mouth piece, put a clipper to his nose and started breathing in the stored oxygen. Two minutes went by and Daring Devon looked up to look at his captain, but to his surprise it was his enemies the gummi bears.

As Brandon blended his factual account of the respiratory experiment with Daring Devon's fantasy world, he was able to communicate his excitement about the physiology research. Harold Rosen's work discusses the type of fictionalizing Brandon was doing. He says we don't just tell the story of our experiences, instead "we invent the experience, the actors, the action, the circumstances, the provocations and the outcomes" (1984, 15). Ultimately, says Rosen, "The 'facts' are reorganized so that what happened becomes what might happen; in this way fiction encompasses and extends the possibilities of human experience." So Brandon's description of measuring respiration becomes more than just a recapitulation of events. It becomes a tense moment in which there are elements of suspense and danger:

> Daring was inhaling the O_2 contaminated with CO_2 for ten minutes. He found it harder to breathe, his throat was dry, and he could feel his head pounding like someone was inflating a balloon in his head, and it was about to pop. As eleven minutes dragged by, they ordered him to stop. Daring found himself drenched with sweat. As he looked up he found out he was no longer in his world but. . . .

While Brandon had trouble writing a typical scientific report, his story included all the sections generally found in such a report. He was able to write the story in the narrative format because each section became an important detail for moving the story forward. The artificial distinctions between the parts were eliminated, and Brandon was able to see how all the parts went together, each one flowing naturally from the previous one. The story form helped Brandon to communicate about the experiment in a way that he and his fellow students could fully understand.

Still, when we read Brandon's story in class, Tia told us that he had left out several parts of the experiment. When Brandon was asked about this later, he said he hadn't worked on those parts of the experiment, so they hadn't seemed like they were part of his story. He began to realize, however, that his story was just his personal view of what had happened. Other students observed that often our points of view limit our reporting of scientific events.

As people discussed Brandon's paper further, the strengths and the limitations of storytelling came to light. It appeared that no story could be entirely complete when it only presented one narrative view. There always seemed to be more to the story that the listeners both could and needed to add. Rosen says the relationship the story-listener and the story-teller have is "always interchangeable, always a collaboration" (1984, 25). In fact, as Tia suggested, it is very important to realize that every story is biased and incomplete. Or, as Rosen, citing R. L. Gregory, put it, "the success of science shows the power of hypotheses as fictions of limited truth" (1984, 17). The students began to realize, as Rosen suggests, that one person telling one story is far too limited a truth. To overcome this limitation, more and more students offered their stories as a way to complete everyone's understanding of just what really was happening in the SSI program.

Brandon's story was only one small part of the research that the exercise physiology students were doing. Beyond the fundamentals of actually conducting the research, Tia saw a larger ethical question: Why do such research at all? In her story, she tried to communicate to the other students why she believed doing this research was important to humanity.

Earlier in the program, Tia's exercise physiology research group had gone to visit a cardial rehabilitation center. While there, the students had interviewed patients. Tia's story was about the patient she interviewed:

> Bob had been sick all his life, he would just lay around all day. His chest was in constant pain. At one of his check ups, he was told he needed a new heart. The hard part was to find a good heart for him. He was put on a waiting list.

By talking with a cardial rehabilitation patient, Tia was able to see what that patient's life was like and why cardial research was important. She was also able to see why other people thought it was necessary work:

> The next heart that was available was too big. The doctors decided to use it anyway, it wouldn't do much harm. The heart was of a 21 year old male who was in a car accident. Since their own son was already brain dead, his parents chose to donate his heart and to have him live on in someone else.

Tia's story helped her to communicate to the other SSI students the human context for work in exercise physiology:

> Bob woke up three days later in the hospital. He felt great. He could feel no more pains in his chest.
>
> Bob took this chance with heart surgery because he had been in pain all his life, and if he died, he would be in no more pain. If he lived, it would only make a new life for him.
>
> He now believes that he is two years old and enjoys his new life to the fullest.
>
> Just hearing how heart transplants save and make better lives for people has made me more aware.

Tia's story illustrated the social dimension of exercise physiology research. Ordinarily, Tia might simply have told a friend or two that she went on a neat field trip to a research lab. But by writing and sharing a story about the experience, she was able to pass on to other students what had really made the experience so meaningful.

Tia and Brandon's stories got at the issues of how and why people do science. Yet the real goal of SSI was not simply to get students to understand the purposes and practicalities of doing science, it was to make them believe that they could become scientists. For this reason, we decided to share Clarice's story with all of our classes. In her story, Clarice demonstrated the shift from only being an observer of science, to actually being a scientist.

Clarice chose to write about a scientific discovery she had made the previous summer while working with "14 slightly chauvinistic men" in the electronics department of a professional research laboratory. In her story, she told about how being a scientist involves more than performing experiments or even wanting to help people. It involves overcoming prejudice and criticism:

> This is the scenario: I was a measly woman, and a high school student at that, what could I accomplish? Would I break down and cry if I screwed up? How could I possibly comprehend this manly field?
>
> So there I was, unwanted by my supervisors.

We had wanted our students to write about a scientific discovery they had made. Clarice's story was about science, but as it unfolded it became a tale of self-discovery:

> One job after the next, my superiors began to realize that not only did I comprehend the art of electronics but I also strove to do something more complex and challenging. After that,

everyone wanted to supervise me so I could do their technical work like drilling, measuring, etc.

Soon enough they all decided that they could find some kind of glitch in my work. So they threw me the ultimate: to build (from scratch) and operate an Argon Liquid Level Detector.

Well, by this time my sentiments were no longer as confident and adamant. I mean, come on, it *was* an Argon Liquid Level Detector!

But then I remembered my diseased stereotype and I willed myself to go on. I could beat this—I knew I could.

In her story, Clarice constantly struggled against all those people who told her she couldn't be a scientist because she was young or because she was female or because she was Hispanic:

This experience left me with the knowledge of the discouraging and dangerous factors associated with stereotypes. Discouraging because if I hadn't been so adamant I would've given up. Dangerous because what if I had connected the wrong wires? hee hee . . .

In the end, Clarice's story let her say: "I am a scientist; I actively affect the world around me; listen up because I have things to say."

In his commentary on science education, Walker Percy moves teachers to reflect on what sense of agency students have in science classrooms.

The tourist who carves his initials in a public place, which is theoretically "his" in the first place, has good reasons for doing so, reasons which the exhibitor and planner know nothing about. He does so because in his role of consumer of an experience (a "recreational experience" to satisfy a "recreational need") he knows that he is disinherited. He is deprived of his title over being. He knows very well that he is in a very special sort of zone in which his only rights are the rights of a consumer. He moves like a ghost through schoolroom, city streets, trains, parks, movies. He carves his initials as a last desperate measure to escape his ghostly role of consumer. He is saying in effect: I am not a ghost after all; I am a sovereign person. And he establishes title the only way remaining to him, by staking his claim over one square inch of wood or stone. (Percy 1991, 62)

Are we leading our students through laboratory experiences and textbook readings, allowing them to be "ghosts" without giving them the opportunity to be sovereign persons, individuals who wish to make their mark in the world of scientific inquiry? The classroom storytelling done by Clarice, Tia, and Brandon required those students to take on the role of scientist rather than taking the tour Percy describes. When students are allowed to write and read science as a story, they are able to lay claim to knowledge, to stake it out for themselves.

Stories are an effective way of preserving and inspiring scientific learning. They offer a way for students to connect what they already understand about the way the world works to the new information they gain from experimentation and investigation. Stories allow students to voice their new and growing understandings. If we want our science students to be inquirers rather than the "tourists" that Percy describes, then we need to provide tools for them to access and communicate their understandings. Roger Schank's work in artificial intelligence led him to discover the connection between intellectual growth and storytelling:

> It helps us to find out what we are currently thinking when we tell a new story, what we used to think when we tell an old one, and what we think of what we think when we hear what we ourselves have to say. (Schank 1990, 146)

Schank claims that we learn from our experience and the experiences of others. It follows that we should teach cases of experience by telling stories and encourage our students to apply such cases to new situations so that they too can tell their stories. In this way, knowledge is shared and built in the community of the scientific classroom.

While teaching reading in the Summer Science Institute, we encountered students who wanted to tell stories and to read science as a story. Because the institute required them to be more than tourists, they had to establish their voices in the scientific community. They became storytellers, narrators of their new experiences. These student scientists read scientific inquiry as an unfolding story and wrote themselves into the plot.

References

Bruner, J. 1988. Research Currents: Life as Narrative. *Language Arts* 65: 575–83.

———. 1990. *Acts of Meaning.* Cambridge, MA: Harvard University Press.

Gould, J. L., and Gould, C. G. 1989. *Life at the Edge: Readings from Scientific American.* New York: W. H. Freeman Company.

Hubbell, S. 1987. *A Country Year: Living the Questions.* New York: Perennial Library.

Leopold, A. 1966. *A Sand County Almanac.* New York: Ballantine Books.

Mason, C. L., Kahle, J. B., and Gardner, A. L. 1991. Draw-a-Scientist Test: Future Implications. *School Science and Mathematics.* 91: 193–98.

McPhee, J. 1976. Travels in Georgia. In *The John McPhee Reader,* edited by W. L. Howarth. New York: Farrar, Straus and Giroux, 267–308.

Percy, W. 1991. *Signposts in a Strange Land.* New York: Farrar, Straus and Giroux.

Rosen, H. 1984. *Stories and Meanings.* London: NATE.

Schank, R. 1990. *Tell Me a Story: A New Look at Real and Artificial Memory.* New York: Macmillan.

10 Teaching on the Frontier: Language and Science

David E. Goodney and Carol S. Long
Willamette University

I define a scientific classic to be a work that has far-reaching effects on the scientific community and society. It doesn't necessarily have to cross all fields; for instance, the discovery of DNA was revolutionary, but had no effect on physics. Also the work must be literarily excellent. Origin of Species was not the first piece on evolution, but certainly the most memorable.

This passage from the journal of a student in our course, "The Literature of Natural Science," reflects the student's attempt to apply techniques of literary analysis to significant scientific texts. The course was developed as an interdisciplinary offering in the General Education program at Willamette University. Such courses, according to the Willamette catalogue, "focus on the process of integrating and using knowledge to develop critical thinking, informed judgment, and sensitivity to the complexities of contemporary... life." Designed and taught by two faculty members from the Chemistry and English departments, "The Literature of Natural Science" was aimed at junior and senior students with majors in science and the humanities. Students in this course included majors in chemistry, physics, biology, English, and psychology. One chemistry student was so interested in the philosophy and religion of science that he was considering graduate school in the philosophy of science. An English major, who was a talented creative writer, always looked for the creative genius in and behind the text. Likewise, the other students worked from their strengths and interests when analyzing the texts.

Our plan was to read classic texts from the history of science using some elements of literary analysis. We chose our reading list to represent different historical periods, different sciences, and several forms of discourse. Taught first in fall, 1985, and again in spring, 1991, the course included texts such as Galileo Galilei's *Dialogue Concerning the Two Chief World Systems*, Sir Isaac Newton's *Mathematical Principles of Natural Philosophy and His System of the World*, Charles Darwin's

Origin of Species, Albert Einstein's *The Meaning of Relativity* and *Relativity,* Steven Weinberg's *The First Three Minutes,* Stephen Hawking's *A Brief History of Time,* as well as excerpts or papers from Robert Boyle (primarily *The Sceptical Chymist*), Francis Bacon (*Novum Organum* and *The New Atlantis*), and Barbara McClintock ("The Origin and Behavior of Mutable Loci in Maize").

The college-wide expectation of these inter-area courses is that upper-level students will make use of their disciplinary backgrounds in pursuing interdisciplinary studies, and we tried to create ways for this to occur. Science majors brought greater understanding of scientific concepts and mathematical language, while literature majors were familiar with metaphor and its function and could talk about voice and structure in the text. Both types of students were able to analyze scientific argument; though they might have studied argumentation in different contexts, all had ideas about allowable and successful tools of argumentation.

Teaching Strategies

We have been fortunate to have small groups in this class (8–12) and have therefore been able to run it in a collaborative seminar format. We feel that many of the techniques used here could generalize to larger groups.

We gave no examinations, relying instead on a combination of papers and journal writing, class presentations, and discussion to help students integrate the materials of the class. Writing assignments included four five-page essays in which we encouraged various forms of analysis. After reading Galileo, students were asked to evaluate the dialogue as a tool for presenting ideas. Other paper topics asked students to discuss the popularizing techniques used by Einstein in *Relativity,* the use of metaphor in Darwin or his views on natural selection, or the student's concept of a "classic of science" in relation to Hawking or McClintock. These topics were all the focus of class discussion before and after their completion and thus developed in a lively group environment rather than in isolation.

In our second experience with the course, we attempted to support student writing through the use of journals. We encouraged students to write responses to their reading and periodically suggested topics for their deliberation. For instance, while reading Darwin, students were asked to identify and discuss techniques of argument; while reading Hawking, students discussed voice in the text. Some students used the journals successfully to develop ideas of their own throughout the semester; for example, the student who was interested in the relationship between science and religion addressed this issue with each text and developed working ideas for his final paper in the context of the journal. His ideas in the journal ranged widely over the relation between science and other fields:

> In general, I would say that the average person believes that science is capable of providing a definite description of the universe and that the findings of science are absolute. When science becomes perceived in this way, I think that negative implications result. Religiously, I think people become weak-minded because they think that science provides all the ultimate answers. It's a material world. Why bother to think about such questions when science supposedly provides all of the answers? Philosophy dies a similar death. . . . There appears to be a difficulty for people to find meaning in both religion and science. I think the split has become too large. Somehow we need to ensure that both retain their meaning.

Other students used the journal in a more eclectic fashion, simply recording immediate responses to the texts, but even for these students the journal was a means of assimilating ideas. We read the journals at three points during the semester and gave written responses to the students. In a large class, response might necessarily be more limited.

In addition to short essays and journals, students presented a final paper that involved additional research. Because this research was interdisciplinary in nature, we felt some help from the library would be useful. We are fortunate to have a library staff well-experienced in offering library instruction. They prepared a preliminary handout on library resources and presented an hour-long class session covering techniques of interdisciplinary research. Students who were familiar with research techniques in literature, philosophy, or science were able to find out about specialized resources in other fields. Science students were perhaps surprised to find Einstein listed in *Contemporary Authors;* humanities students were interested to discover the Q section in the library and works such as *Information Sources in the History of Science and Medicine.* All were intrigued to learn of the many entries concerning science in the *Encyclopedia of Religion* or of the adaptation of particular words in the needs of science as documented in the *Oxford English Dictionary.*

Such library training led to stronger papers as well as to an awareness of potential resources for later reading and study. Reserve materials were also useful in this respect. Historical or contextual information about the period of a work or about nonscientific concerns of the authors we studied was of particular interest. Students must be able easily and comfortably to access historical, social, biographical, and scientific background information so they can appreciate the richness of each text.

We sometimes asked students to make class presentations either to provide background for their reading or to make their own ideas more formally available to the rest of the class. The most successful of these were closely tied to their reading or their paper writing. For example, each student was asked to present a summary of one chapter of Darwin's *Origin;* though Darwin himself provides a good number of summaries within the text, this exercise seemed helpful to the students in recognizing the logical progression of Darwin's argument. We also asked each student to make a presentation on his or her final paper to promote discussion by the class.

Class discussion was sometimes challenging to manage, but we were aided by the use of journal topics and by specified reading for each class session. Defining a "classic of science" was also an aid to early discussion; most students had existing opinions as to what constituted a classic, and it was a term that allowed us to begin the conversation about different expectations within the various disciplines. One senior English major (our creative writer) invented a conversation between Shakespeare (Bill), Einstein (Al), Galileo (George), and Darwin (Chuck) about the nature of the classic:

> *Bill:* . . . every piece of literature need not appeal to the masses, but they must understand it if they are to enjoy it.

> *George:* Very good point. But you forget, Al's idea was very forward and new, much in the same vein as my work. The only difference was that Al was not being contested by the church.

> *Chuck:* Are you saying then, that a piece considered blasphemous or detrimental to God is a classic? If that is the case my friend, then I am a lock for candidacy into this elite club of classic authors.

Literature students expected longevity and relevance from a classic; science students were more apt to see the classic as "outdated."

We also used our knowledge of student backgrounds in early discussion, directing questions to those who might have previous knowledge of a subject. We could always return to the text to ask about specific textual questions or interpretations. During the semester we encouraged students to develop particular interests of their own in relation to the texts, and this meant that discussion was on the whole more successful in the latter part of the semester when the people particularly interested in science and religion could respond to each other, or when we could direct questions about metaphor to the student who was focusing on metaphor in the texts.

Textual Strategies

Aside from these general teaching strategies centered around discussion and paper-writing, we also approached the course with an agenda related to reading and the nature of discourse. We hoped to demonstrate to ourselves and our students that we could analyze scientific texts and learn something new about them by reading with an eye to elements such as structure, metaphor, voice, and techniques of argumentation. We introduced our ideas about the study of the literature of natural science and discussed some of the difficulties of such a study in a previous article in the *Willamette Journal of the Liberal Arts* where we concluded that "The works of science can be studied like other types of literature within a consistent intellectual framework" (Goodney and Long 1988, 76). Based on our definition of a classic in science, we chose the texts for the course using the criteria of truth, accessibility, form, and impact, categories suggested in part by Derek Gjertsen's work, *The Classics of Science* (1984). Reading the texts themselves was emphasized throughout the class.

The reading of texts has different meanings for scientists and humanists. For a scientist the content is paramount and style incidental, while for a humanist much of the meaning is in the style. So one of the challenges of this course is to teach different ways of reading. Science students must learn to read critically to see how style, form, or structure helps understanding. Humanities students, on the other hand, must see past formal style and jargon to appreciate the meaning. Both types of students can use their strengths to help the comprehension of others through class discussions. The different perspectives interact synergistically for understanding the text. For all students, one of the results of our reading was the demythologizing of science. Those with a strong background in science saw the linguistic and social context of scientific inquiry more clearly; those with a background in language were enabled to approach technical texts with more assurance.

The semester began with an introduction to rhetorical theory and theory of discourse, which provided a framework for the course.

Students read selections from James L. Kinneavy's *A Theory of Discourse* (1971), Walter R. Fisher's *Human Communication as Narration* (1987), and Diane Macdonnell's *Theories of Discourse: An Introduction* (1986). Kinneavy suggests that "A discourse which becomes noticeably expressive or directly persuasive or literarily preoccupied is a discourse which is in danger of becoming nonscientific" (1991, 88). It was on this boundary between science and other discourse that we spent much of our time. At the end of the semester the theories of discourse allowed us to summarize and synthesize our rather disparate texts.

We approached the study of texts by asking, "What does the literature of natural science hope to accomplish and how?" A simple, but not simplistic, answer to this first question is that the literature of natural science tries to communicate scientific observations and theories. Avoiding for now the philosophical implications of this answer, we can observe that the second question is more interesting and pertinent to our course. In this light, scientific writing is an argumentative essay; facts (data) are collected, organized, and presented to support a particular conclusion (theory). It was our intent to analyze the rhetorical devices and conventions of scientific writing as argumentative essay. It is often in frontier science, classics that change science, that the argumentative form is most apparent.

The form and style of modern scientific writing often obscure its intent as an argumentative essay under the guise of a factual report. Indeed, students in science classes are often taught the stereotypical scientific style with its third person, impersonal pronouns, and passive verbs when writing laboratory reports for undergraduate science courses. No wonder students don't read original scientific reports! This stereotype contains an element of truth, but also fosters misunderstandings. We attempted to remove scientific writing from the shadows of obscurity and to illuminate it through literary criticism.

Significantly, several of the texts we read (Galileo, Newton, Darwin, Einstein) were the basis of scientific revolutions in the sense of Thomas Kuhn. Analysis of the forms of argument in these texts was, therefore, especially interesting. As Kuhn points out in *The Structure of Scientific Revolutions*, the revolution is not carried by the science alone, but also by "arguments, rarely made entirely explicit, that appeal to the individual's sense of the appropriate or the aesthetic . . ." (1970, 155). We intended for students not only to observe differences between revolutionary science and normal science, but also to speculate on the function of humor in Galileo's *Dialogue* and thought experiments in Einstein's *Relativity.* Because we read the texts in chronological order, we were also able to have students observe some interesting historical trends: use of the dialogue in the seventeenth century; increasing specialization; and the rise of the "paper." But to understand these trends we needed to put the works within a historical, social, and philosophical context. We included enough discussion of the history of science, sociology of science, and philosophy of science so that students would understand the way science works and how it has changed. Thus, in spite of the difficulty of the individual texts, the students could evaluate them as elements within the larger picture.

Textual Examples

Certainly the analysis of a scientific text is different than that of a novel or poem, but not much different than the analysis of an essay. The elements of style we explored included voice, vocabulary, metaphor, and structure, as well as assumptions about scientific paradigm and audience. We discovered that it was easier to apply literary categories to earlier works of science where the distinction between literary and scientific styles was less clear. For example, the students were pleasantly surprised to discover the dialogue format, with its characterization as used successfully by Galileo and less successfully by Boyle.

Galileo's *Dialogue* was an attractive opening text because of its many interesting and accessible techniques. His descriptions of observations and experiments and his use of believable characterization enlivened the reading and held the students' attention. The history of Galileo's relation to the church and his relation to other scientists working on similar problems provided interesting background; modern works such as Brecht's play *Galileo* could be used as adjunct readings to add personality and historical perspective. The text also provided us with a reason for looking back at the science of Aristotle so that we could expand the historical range of the course slightly.

Discussion of the characters in the text and the ways in which they functioned to advance Galileo's argument proved interesting. Simplicio was both amusing and sympathetic and provided an occasion for discussion of belief systems. Asked to comment on Galileo's use of dialogue in the journal, one student wrote:

> Most obviously the dialogue allows Galileo to present his views through "characters." These figures had the ability to discuss more controversial ideas than Galileo could have in the first person. Another advantage of the dialogue is the opportunity to discuss opposing views.

Asked to analyze the characters of the dialogue, another student wrote:

> I find Salviati, Sagredo, and Simplicio an interesting mix of personalities. Salviati is the "learned one," he is a master of science and reasoning. . . . I see him as a grizzled old professor, stubborn through experience and extremely wise . . . Simplicio is just that, a simple person but not a simple mind. He seems to be a learned priest-like character. Very knowledgeable about Aristotle, but yet reveres him with faith. Aristotle's words are never questioned, only reapplied deductively to a situation.

In our second experience with this course, the students were so taken with the dialogue form that two of them wrote their final papers in dialogue structure, one in a very close parallel to Galileo.

We also discussed Galileo's purpose in choosing the dialogue form, which led us to consider the evolution of a scientific style and to discuss the nature of the scientific community in Galileo's time. The dialogue also introduced the possibility of subterfuge, with Galileo presenting his own ideas in the mouth of a fictional character and attempting to avoid direct confrontation with the church by couching his argument in an indirect and ingenious style. Through his use of the vernacular language and the dialogue format, Galileo raised many provocative questions about an author's choice of style, relation to convention, and sense of audience.

This question of audience was also important to another of our authors, Charles Darwin. His text too was a relatively successful one, although there were chapters in which the detailed evidence presented seemed to be discouraging to some readers. Darwin is typical both of natural history writers in his attention to detail and of Victorian writers with complex sentence structure and extended metaphor. We were fortunate that many of our students had taken Willamette's first-year student interdisciplinary seminar, "World Views," which for four years had included a reading from Darwin, so some of them were meeting the *Origin* for the second time. One student remarked in his journal:

> It's only been a year since World Views, and I have already [met] Darwin again. Actually I enjoyed his *Origin of Species* more this time than previous opportunities. . . . I believe I understood his theory of natural selection far better, and the intricacies of arguing his points.

This experience of studying a text several times with different priorities in mind helped students to see various purposes and levels in the work. The dramatic context of Darwin's ideas and the history of his own travels, as well as the still unfolding discussion concerning evolution, all helped to keep students involved in the text. Here again the relationship between religion and science was of interest, and we studied the text in terms of word choice and argumentative statements to see how questions of religion were dealt with.

Darwin does not create characters in a dialogue, but he does create a very clear persona who attempts to build credibility, who is thorough and logical, and who uses many different argumentative techniques in persuading the audience. One of his most successful ploys is to engender a sympathetic identification between audience and persona and then to show how he himself was persuaded gradually of his own conclusions.

In contrast to Darwin, twentieth-century scientists adopt an impersonal style, which enables us to discuss changes in the conventions of scientific discourse. The trend toward increased specialization has changed the audience for scientific writing; most is inaccessible to the layperson. Attempting to read a scientific paper quickly teaches a student why only "experts" read the original literature. Yet students should make the attempt, if only to analyze the structure of the scientific paper. In contrast to the paper is the book by a "popularizer," intended for a general audience. Increasingly, popular books are written by the experts themselves. The students were able to compare directly technical and popular works by two authors, Einstein and Hawking.

The modern genre of the paper was represented in our course by the writing of Barbara McClintock. Her career is interesting because she is a woman scientist in a predominantly male field, and her work could not be appreciated by the scientific community until the discovery of molecular genetics. In spite of the catch phrase "jumping genes," her contribution, though of Nobel Prize stature, is largely unknown outside of biology.

One reason her work remains largely unknown is her decision to write only technical papers; others must translate her work to a wider audience. When reading her technical papers, students are intimidated by the jargon and density of the argument. Even science majors unfamiliar with gene theory found her work difficult. As one chemistry student wrote in his journal:

> Her articles on maize and the transposition of genes were very confusing. The terminology involved was so obscure that it made for little comprehension. . . . McClintock's article is very dry and unfeeling. She put none of her personality into the article. In fact, she refers to herself in the neuter.

The jargon and the density of the argument are both common features of the modern scientific paper. Yet the seeming incomprehensibility provides an opportunity for an interesting exercise, analysis of the form alone of a scientific argument. And typical of scientific arguments, data are presented with warnings about their limitations, arguments are constructed with hedge words like "could" or "might," and no matter how strongly a conclusion is held, it is presented as provisional. These argumentative traits were particularly apparent to students near the end of the course when they had had experience analyzing other styles of argument in science.

Although Barbara McClintock's words on paper seem dry, her image on video reveals an interesting personality. Students who reacted negatively to the papers were enchanted by her story in a PBS documentary. Indeed, many wondered why she did not write in a fashion that would let her personality come through. It seems that scientists are also captives of the prevailing style, a style which is two-dimensional rather than three-dimensional art.

A direct comparison of the prevailing technical style with a more popular exposition was provided by the reading of Einstein's *The Meaning of Relativity* (1974) and *Relativity: The Special and the General Theory* (1961). Different stylistic and rhetorical devices appear in these two works, one a classic argumentative essay in science and the other an understandable explication for a general audience. Einstein's theory of relativity was originally published over a period of years as journal articles. The technical version is an integration and expansion of the papers and, thus, a bridge between the monograph and the paper.

The most obvious feature of the technical version is the extensive use of mathematics requiring a knowledge of tensor calculus to follow the proofs. Interestingly, the equations, which are essential to the theory, are integrated within the text, often as part of a sentence. Indeed, unlike Newton's *Principia*, there is more text than mathematics and the logical form of the argument can easily be followed, even by those without a background in calculus. An even closer examination of the text shows Einstein explaining the proofs and their consequences in words:

> If we apply the last of equations (43) to a material particle at rest (q = o), we see that the energy, E, of a body at rest is equal to its mass. Had we chosen the second as our unit of time, we would have obtained (44) $E = mc^2$. Mass and energy are therefore alike: they are only different expressions for the same thing. (46–47)

Thus students may find reading this version of *Relativity* unsatisfying because they cannot follow the mathematics, but they will not find it incomprehensible. The popular version is, however, quite satisfying for most students. The use of mathematics has been reduced, although it is still incorporated into the text. Einstein introduces his famous thought experiment of "a railway carriage which is travelling uniformly..." and carries it through the book as his metaphor for motion. As one student reported in his journal:

> I found the non-mathematic edition of the *General Theory of Relativity* to be quite interesting. What made it easier to understand was the consistency of his use of the same model. For instance, the train kept on reoccurring. This made it simpler to connect the ideas from each chapter and string them together.

The arguments in the popular version are sustained by the train plus a variety of other thought experiments drawn from common experience. Students follow the arguments and willingly accept even the most outrageous conclusions of relativity!

Assessment and Reflection

As a result of this course, we believe that indeed it is possible to teach scientific texts as literature within limits and that such reading and analysis are beneficial for the students. Humanities students discover that their skill with language is transferrable from one discipline to another and that they are able to approach scientific texts with understanding. Science students learn more about the history of science and the nature of language used in the pursuit of science. All students learn more about the social and linguistic context of scientific enterprise. Our discussions about style, voice, character, and metaphor demonstrate to student readers the variety of techniques used in science writing throughout history. We could then talk about the levels of persuasion that are used to prove a theory successfully in scientific discourse.

The results of the course are best illustrated in one of the final papers submitted by a biology student who wrote a dialogue patterned after Galileo, even maintaining the names of Galileo's characters, but discussing genetic transposition. The dialogue is set in Cold Spring Harbor after a seminar presented there by McClintock, and three scientists are discussing the seminar. The student not only used Galileo's characters, but also attempted to parallel his use of analogy and metaphor in the argument.

Salv.: In order to illustrate the difference in the need for controlling mechanisms between single-celled prokaryotes and multicellular eukaryotic organisms I would like to propose an example. Simplicio, suppose you owned a factory and this factory consisted of one room with ten machines. Each machine is different from the others and can only produce one product. This factory is completely automated and operates twenty-four hours a day. As the owner you do not want to waste energy and resources producing a product that is not needed. How could you prevent this from occurring?

Later in the dialogue Sagredo enters the discussion with Simplicio:

Sagr.: So Simplicio, do you still believe that a simple inducer or repressor system can work in multicellular organisms?

Simp.: Wait, I'm thinking about this. They could still work if all the other genes were somehow permanently turned off and couldn't respond to the inducer.

Still later Salviati and Sagredo come up with a metaphor to explain the operation of transposition:

Salv.: Well suppose someone went around to all our factories and shoved a wrench in the gears of every Machine C except those in the ten factories we want C produced in. This would mean that all the machines would be disabled as you requested and only our ten factories would be able to respond to the message.

Sagr.: So what you are saying is that there is a genetic wrench in every insulin gene in the body except those located in the pancreas.

The student ended the dialogue with some pithy remarks on the nature of science:

Salv.: Remember it is only the model and our understanding of it that has changed, not the true nature of the organism. When our current model impairs our understanding and holds us back from scientific progress, it is time for it to be changed.

Simp.: Perhaps you are right.

This project represents an interesting blend of the student's previous knowledge with the things learned in the class and also illustrates an adaptation of an earlier style of scientific writing to the circumstances of contemporary science.

On the whole we felt that the tools of textual analysis were successful in bringing together students from the sciences and the humanities over the discussion of scientific texts. The common medium of language was a useful bridge between student specialists who were able to pursue questions of mutual interest in a collaborative setting.

Acknowledgments

We would like to express our thanks to the students who joined us in this course and especially those whose works are quoted in this essay.

References

Fisher, W. R. 1987. *Human Communication as Narration.* Columbia: Univ. of South Carolina Press.

Gjertsen, D. 1984. *The Classics of Science.* New York: Lilian Barber Press, Inc.

Goodney, D., and C. Long. 1988. The Literature of Natural Science. *Willamette Journal of the Liberal Arts.* Supplemental Series 2: 59–78.

Kinneavy, J. L. 1971. *A Theory of Discourse.* New York: Norton.

Kuhn, T. S. 1970. *The Structure of Scientific Revolutions.* 2d ed. Chicago: Univ. of Chicago Press.

Macdonnell, D. 1986. *Theories of Discourse: An Introduction.* Cambridge, Mass.: Basil Blackwell.

11 Spiders, Fireflies, and the Glow of Popular Science

Roy F. Fox
University of Missouri

I chose a poem about insects," I told the group of twelve people who had turned out at dusk in Horseshoe Bend, Idaho, to discuss a book of poetry with me.

"It's on page 220."

The eleven women, all gray-haired, and one man, a retired rancher silently accompanying his wife, quietly shifted their chairs, shuffled pages, and settled down to follow the words as I spoke them aloud:

Fireflies

Now there are no fireflies. Once
there were, and we caught them.
Children, our white sweaters glinting
in the dusk, chasing after other children.
They seemed that way, children
or the very old, dottering in slow flight.
We'd charge any flash and wait
at arms' length for one another. And always,
there was. Once we kept them
in an unwashed honey jar, three dozen
snagged and flickering on the oozy sides.
Carefully we plucked each away and wrote
with the smear of their phosphorescence
our names on a stone wall,
and afterward licked our fingers,
and they were sweet and golden.

—Robert Wrigley

Unlike my other library talks, I had not looked forward to this meeting. Horseshoe Bend is a small lumber mill town, whose library was hosting a series of book discussions, "Let's Talk about It," sponsored by the state library. I'd been told by last month's discussion leader that the regulars at these things didn't like the previous novel in the

---

series, so I was positive they'd hate an entire book of *poems* even more.

I decided to ask participants to read their favorite poems aloud to the group and then to explain why they chose their poem. I justified this approach by reminding them of oral and communal traditions, where groups gathered to share stories and poems.

What we were going to do tonight, I assured them, began far, far back into the mists of time—when the Nez Perce told and retold myths and legends; when mothers, fathers, and grandparents told stories around campfires—heat warming the body, narrative warming the spirit; when parents hummed and sang lowly into the face of a high infant mortality rate to calm their children and themselves; when medicine men chanted into a spread of cold stars.

Finally, I pointed to the book's introduction by William Stafford, who asks, "How can we enter that cavern of realization that Native Americans . . . felt when they used sound to interact with mystery?" Yes, even if I had to drag them, we were all going to use sound to interact with mystery.

It worked. People read like blazes. They were interested in each other's selections and why and how the poems had been chosen. Although the retired rancher, attentive throughout, "passed" on reading aloud, several people wanted two turns, so they could speak their second-favorite poem.

I was the last to read. When I'd finished, looking up from the page, the women stared back at me in silence, with as much of a puzzled look on their faces as mature people ever have. Somehow, I picked up on their hesitation and waited for them to talk.

"Aren't fireflies mythical beings?" one woman asked.

"No . . . I don't believe so," another woman said quietly, "we had them in Pennsylvania years ago."

"What do they look like?"

"You mean they really glow? Like a real light?"

"What makes them live in some parts of the country and not in others?"

We talked for twenty minutes about what we knew of fireflies. And more importantly, what we didn't know. Seven of the twelve people, who had lived their entire lives in the arid West, had never seen a firefly. I chose this poem, I told them, because I used to capture "lightning bugs" in a jar in Missouri. I even felt safe enough to tell them about my rare sightings of blue fireflies and wondered if they were mutants. I told them how I've never found another human being to corroborate this phenomenon—how other people usually think one of my computer chips is dimming.

"Maybe," one woman gently ventured, "the glass you were looking through made them just *look* like they were blue, not yellow."

"No, I don't really think so. . . . Hold on here—*you* don't believe me, either, do you? But I still insist they're out there. In fact, last summer in the Ozarks, I spotted a blue one outside my bedroom window and went outside to see it directly. It was blue, alright."

And so went our discussion. We shared knowledge and treated our ignorance casually. Somehow, in spite of my evangelism, we really had used sound—language—to interact with mystery. And once ignited, it didn't burn out easily or quickly: Several months later, I ran across Howard Ensign Evans' "In Defense of Magic: The Story of Fireflies" (1968). Recalling my evening in Horseshoe Bend, I devoured the chapter in a flash. It didn't answer all of our group's questions, but some of them. And it raised and answered a lot more questions we didn't think about.

Evans' language helps this mystery make sense. And even though he is an experienced and knowledgeable scientist, his words express the same wonder about fireflies that we experienced in our discussion that night in rural Idaho.

This happens, I believe, because all of us—the people at the library, myself, Evans (the writing entomologist), the chanting medicine men, the grief-stricken, the grown-ups who tell stories to children—use language to interact with mysteries. The people at the library chose their own mysteries in poems, as I did when I selected the one about fireflies. And through language, the awe we feel about our respective mysteries is more naturally, clearly, and emphatically communicated to others, who, in turn, have their own curiosity sparked by the sharing.

This is the stuff of Evans' article. It is the stuff of all superb popular science writing, which is why teachers of many disciplines and levels, from biology to art, from junior high school to college, should ask their students to select a mystery (which is somehow relevant to the course) and write a descriptive popular science article about it.

The process of writing popular science, of making a mystery make sense for a naive reader, immerses students in what is best about science: commitment, curiosity, discovery, focus, precision, knowledge, and facts. At the same time, students are absorbed in what is best about the humanities: commitment, exploration, creativity, and clear communication motivated only for purposes of sharing information. Writing a popular science article integrates "the two cultures" as few activities can.

I call the assignment, "Make a Mystery Make Sense," and I've used it mainly with college undergraduates, though it can be easily adapted to other levels. I introduce the project by telling students the same story about fireflies I began this chapter with. Or, I begin with some other "author's story"—some convoluted journey guided only by passionate, personal interest, such as E. B. White's curiosity about spiders, which led him to write the children's classic, *Charlotte's Web*.

Although White thoroughly researched spiders by reading, among other works, John Henry Comstock's *Spider Book* and by consulting with an expert at the American Museum of Natural History, he only pursued the subject because he'd become entranced by the spiders living in his own barn in Maine. So I often share this account with students, telling them how, one cold October day, White, from atop a stepladder, with an extension light in hand, quietly watched *Aranea cavatica* spin an egg sac and deposit her eggs. A few days later, not wanting to miss anything due to a trip to New York, White took a razor blade and carefully extracted the spider and sac from the barn's roof, gently placed them into a candy box, and "carried them to town." Once in Manhattan, he tossed the box onto his bedroom dresser and forgot about it. Weeks later, though, he found "Charlotte's daughters" coming out of the air holes he'd punched in the lid:

> They strung tiny lines from my comb to my brush, from my brush to my mirror, and from my mirror to my nail scissors. They were very busy and almost invisible, they were so small. We all lived together happily for a couple of weeks .... (White 1953)

Such an introduction emphasizes the most important element of this assignment—personal, passionate curiosity. Nothing less. And this intense interest in the topic is the assignment's most unbendable requirement.

Although I introduce this assignment during the first week of classes, we do the main work of it near semester's end. This gives students time to decide upon a mystery that they're most interested in and also communicates how seriously I insist upon seriousness. Experienced writers better know their passions, but many student writers don't—and they are precisely the ones who most need to experience the nurture between authentic involvement and effective expression.

During the first month of classes, every couple of days I encourage students to "let me know what you're thinking about" for this assignment, and when time allows, I ask them to do a freewriting telling me about their ideas. About a month after introducing the assignment, I ask students to freewrite about their topic, explaining why and how they're interested in it. This freewriting is in preparation for a peer group sharing of ideas only.

In groups of seven or eight students, each writer orally explains his or her idea. No reading of papers or writing is allowed here; they just get in the way. This impromptu talk allows students to learn what others are planning and shows students ways to change their own ideas. More importantly, within a group of seven or eight students, you're bound to have three or four who will speak of their ideas with contagious excitement, making their energy visible to others who, until now, haven't been able to recognize it. More than anything else, this informal sharing of ideas helps students recognize their topics.

I give final approval of students' topics by talking briefly with them before and after class. My first question is, "Why are you interested in pygmy goats (or left-handedness or llamas)?" In their responses, I listen closely to their words, but I search hardest for one thing: some spark of animation, some tone of voice, some facial expression to convince me that they're excited about the subject. This is my most important criterion for giving them the go-ahead, and it's a completely subjective call on my part. Getting personally acquainted with students *before* you have to make this call, helps—which is another reason to announce the assignment early and actually do it later. Because of the primacy of personal involvement in topics, I usually approve some mysteries that fall outside pure science, but instead are rooted in technology ("How are computers used to design sports cars?") or in the social sciences ("How does the 'office romance' affect productivity?").

When it's time to embark on the actual project, about a month before the end of the semester, I give students a copy of Evans' article. Of course, any model of clear, accessible language will do, from Lewis Thomas, to John McPhee, to Rachel Carson. After we discuss the author's methods for making science appealing, I summarize them as a list of guidelines or tentative evaluation criteria. (The list in the box is based on Evans' article.) These guidelines serve as initial psychological support more than anything else. Once the entire assignment process is nearly complete and students have responded to each other's papers in groups (but not yet completed final revisions), they return

Guidelines for the Make a Mystery Make Sense Assignment
(Based upon "In Defense of Magic: The Story of Fireflies" by Howard Ensign Evans)

1. **Describe your** *whole* subject from a distanced perspective. Mention the whole subject's main parts, but don't go into any detail about them; focus on the *single* entity. *Example:* Evans begins with, "What can rival a twilit meadow rich with the essence of June and spangled with fireflies?"

2. **Explain how your subject is part of something larger,** by placing it into its larger context or natural setting. *Example:* Evans connects fireflies to other life forms (bacteria and coral) and to research about life on other planets. Also link your subject to something larger by answering questions like, "What does it do?" and "What is it for?" *Example:* Evans explains what makes fireflies flash off and on. Finally, try placing your subject into larger categories or groups. *Example:* Evans explains that fireflies are neither flies nor bugs nor worms, but instead are beetles, and only one of many organisms that glow.

3. **Break your subject into its main parts,** stages, components, or features. Label each part, and break it down further. *Example:* Evans breaks his subject into several main parts, including 1) when and why fireflies glow; 2) the history of fireflies; 3) behavior patterns; and 4) communication.

4. **Describe the various parts of your subject.** Focus first on those parts or qualities that make your subject different from other similar items. *Example:* Evans describes fireflies' unique place in human history, how Aristotle and Pliny wrote about them. Use close-up observations, focusing upon details about details. *Example:* Evans states that the firefly's main light organ "contains large, slablike light cells, each of them filled with large granules and much smaller, dark granules, the latter . . . concentrated around the numerous air tubes and nerves . . ." Use examples to show how your topic behaves, appears, or functions, by giving a "for instance." *Example:* "Obviously, some of the more complex animals—fish and insects for instance—have elaborated this primitive light-producing capacity into specialized organs . . ." Use language that appeals to readers' senses of sight, sound, taste, touch, and smell. *Example:* See the quote in #1 above. Use comparisons. *Example:* ". . .when the insect is moving along the ground it looks like nothing so much as a fully lighted railroad train." Use alternative explanations alongside technical terms or jargon. *Example:* Evans states that the scientist who discovered the substances required to produce light "called these two substances luciferin and luciferase (after Lucifer, who among other devilish traits was the bearer of light)." Use terms common for *your* readers. *Example:* What are "lightning bugs" to Americans may be "glowworms" to Europeans. What an Iowa farmer calls a "firebug" may be exactly what an entomologist calls "*Lampyridae.*"

to the initial guidelines to mold their own set of final evaluation criteria, which I then apply to final drafts. Students are not bound to the initial guidelines in any way, though they often use some of them, reworded or verbatim.

Evans' piece primarily describes, which is what I want students to do. I also ask students to aim these articles at a lay or general audience, as Evans does, who chooses his description accordingly, engaging the reader without sacrificing the science behind his discussion. Evans uses description primarily to show how fireflies glow. But he also uses it to touch on the larger issue of nature's "magic" (seemingly concentrated in the firefly's brief flash) that both drives forward and eludes scientific investigation.

Likewise, the description in the piece reflects this tension between what we know and what nature will continue to keep secret from us. And so, when reading Evans' essay, we encounter lush description that evokes nature's mystery, as well as description made up of what is direct, precise, observable. In some places, both types occur almost side by side, and as a result, the general audience reads science that is intellectually challenging, accessible, and delightful.

In addition to describing their mysteries for a general audience, I also ask students to use subheads throughout their piece, a practice which helps them—and their readers—"chunk" and organize complex material. Another option is for students to employ a "Myths/Facts" approach to illuminate their mysteries. This design, also commonly used to communicate complex material to general readers, has a built-in organizational framework.

Here, after some research, students begin by roughly sorting their information into two groups, truth and misconception. After writing "Myth," students clearly state one widely held but false notion about the topic. Next, after writing "Fact," they clearly explain how and why that notion is false, and what the truth is. Each student refutes several of the most common myths about his or her topic.

These myths/facts should follow some sequence, or, if students are dealing with many myths/facts, they should group them into two or three categories. (Some, but not all, of the boxed guidelines also apply to the myths/facts approach.)

However, whether students are writing articles with subheads or articulating their subject's fictions and facts, I often ask them to present their information orally to the class. This eight- to ten-minute presentation, which occurs after their written projects are completed, constitutes a simplified and boiled-down version of their paper.

Although I encourage informality, students decide upon the appropriate room arrangement, whether they should stand behind a podium or sit in a circle, and other details. They have to direct their presentations to an audience who is educated but not knowledgeable about their specific topic. Their talk must include several elements.

First, because they are communicating complex material to a naive audience, students must use two to four visual aids. One of these must be an outline of their talk, composed of three or four highly memorable words or phrases placed on an overhead transparency. These are concrete phrases, puns, rhymes, and other zingers. Each hook should embody a major supporting point of the presenter's talk and hence compress much information. For example, one student who attempted to demystify the effects of television viewing used the phrases, "boob toob," "lewd tube," and "mean screen" to signify his three main supporting points.

I encourage students to illustrate each hook visually, often with simple line drawings or cartoons. Students can also bring in objects to hold and pass around as they explain each phrase or subpoint. While showing each hook, students should ideally "talk it through"— if at all possible, without notes. This is easier if students are authentically interested in their subject and know it well. In communicating these requirements, I explain that this simplifying and compressing of information, delivered informally by an involved speaker, is necessary for communicating new and complex ideas to a general audience— again, the stuff of popular science.

If students present their papers orally, a question-and-answer-session (about three to five minutes) at the end of their talk is also crucial: It satisfies individual curiosities of audience members (which, in turn, often elicits more interest), and it tests the depth of the speaker's knowledge and impromptu thinking. Most questions from the audience arise naturally and spontaneously. These are always the best ones. However, for insurance purposes (and for fun) I sometimes ask students to devise questions from certain points of view found in most general audiences: the person who bores in upon minutiae; the listener who seeks connections with the topic and global concerns; the audience member who makes a statement in the guise of a question; the whiner who won't accept any answer.

When each talk is finished and the next person is setting up, the audience completes a brief freewriting or a response form, indicating what worked well and what could use improvement. I emphasize well ahead of time that these presentations are practice sessions and everyone wants balanced, specific, and practical feedback. Obvious questions are answered, such as, "Did this mystery, by presentation's end, make sense?" "Was specific information clear?" "Did the speaker make *you* interested in the subject?" "Were the hooks and visuals effective?" Audience members write their names in the upper right corner of the sheet, and I collect them to scan after class.

After I quickly read through all of them, I cut off the names and return the stack to the presenter. I also complete a signed evaluation myself, which contains the student's grade for the oral presentation. Most of the time, but not always, these grades reflect an average of what the entire audience thought. Especially for the first few presentations, I monitor the audience comments, devoting the first few minutes of class to reading a few examples of specific, constructive, and positive feedback.

The oral presentations are weighted about half of what a major written assignment would be, usually fifty points. Such an activity should not be overemphasized *or* undervalued. Most students, most of the time, do quite well. They gain knowledge, skill, and confidence, all the while enjoying the variety of mysteries and their peers' involvement in them.

White and Evans write about mysteries of nature, and so do many students. Others are most intrigued by the intricacies of computer technology, physics, engineering, television, astronomy, law, or any other topic that they've developed some kind of organic attachment to. They also must make their topic relevant to the course in some way, sometimes a challenging task, but one that helps them see connections between their interests and the course they're enrolled in.

One hard part of this assignment is determining when students can be pushed upward to a topic that's more of a mystery—and when they can't be. One writer wanted to demystify the creation of a soybean casserole. I gently redirected this student, who finally completed a respectable project on the conundrums of consumer labeling of food products. When necessary, considerations of what represents the most intriguing mystery for the most audience members helps in redirecting student choices.

The hardest part of this assignment is motivating sincere interest and helping students discover one mystery that ignites them. "Perfunctory walk-throughs," I bluntly remind them, "anything—just to fulfill the assignment—won't do." Like in teaching anything, some students never catch fire. Time runs out and I lamely approve their "least perfunctory" choice. But at least they begin to understand that personal fires feed real inquiry, that this heat, too, rises.

Although *how* students come to know their mysteries can be a riddle in itself, they should understand that their success depends heavily on recognizing a topic that fascinates them. *Selection, invention, critical inquiry, passion*—call it what you will, this search for exactly what inflames each of us is the DNA code of the sciences and humanities.

The best work is always born of such passion. Amazingly, we forget this simple truth all the time. In *Charlotte's Web*, E. B. White expresses his own quiet passions about the mystery of nature. When students succeed at writing popular science, what they really assert is both greater and simpler than mere science or humanities. They express the same message as White did, when he responded to a reader who wanted to know the "deep symbolic meanings" in his story about the spider:

> All that I hope to say in books, all that I ever hope to say, is that I love the world. I guess you can find that in there if you dig around. (*Letters of E. B. White*)

References

Evans, H. E. 1968. *Life on a Little-Known Planet.* New York: E.P. Dutton.

White, E. B. 1953. Pigs and Spiders. *McClurg's Book News.* 49.

———. 1952. *Charlotte's Web.* New York: Harper and Row.

———. 1977. *Letters of E. B. White,* Dorothy Guth, Ed. New York: Harper and Row.

12 When Biology Meets English: Health Sciences in the Composition Classroom

Bruce Maylath
University of Minnesota

When you were a student taking science classes, you may have heard something similar to what my tenth-grade biology teacher told my classmates and me. One of us asked if we would receive lower grades on lab reports if we didn't write them well. "This is biology, not English class," the teacher responded. "I don't care how you write, as long as I can see that you understand biology." Even to a fifteen-year-old like me, his statement seemed to divide the sciences from the humanities unnecessarily and perhaps even detrimentally. I recall thinking at the time, "How can you show that you know biology if you don't get your points across well in your writing?"

That was in 1973, and although I didn't know it, the writing across the curriculum movement was just beginning to crawl out of infancy into toddlerhood. Its earliest proponents, notably James Britton and James Moffett, had already made the case that knowledge in any discipline, the sciences included, is assembled and used by means of the symbol system of language. Today, thanks to their efforts and the many who followed them, language across the curriculum programs are under widespread discussion and implementation. Indeed, although some science teachers might still be loath to include much writing in

---

This essay is dedicated to the late Dr. Michael Loupe, professor at the University of Minnesota dentistry school and director of its educational research, planning, and development. Dr. Loupe epitomized the tie between writing and the disciplines being discussed in this book.

their courses, their resistance often proves hollow and grounded more in fear than rationality.

Much to our surprise, those of us involved in language across the curriculum efforts at the University of Minnesota have discovered that our colleagues in the sciences—particularly the health sciences—are in fact often eager to include an integration of language and the humanities with science. What follows is the story of how the health science departments at the University of Minnesota teamed up with the Program in Composition and Communication to provide a writing course featuring instruction in biomedical ethics, as well as written medical formats.

Our efforts to establish a course in "Writing in the Health Sciences" began in 1988. The idea for the course was actually an attempt to meet the professional communication needs of a sizable group of Minnesota science majors. Academic advisors in such fields as nursing, physical and occupational therapy, veterinary sciences, premedicine, and predentistry remarked that the types of writing and subjects addressed in Advanced Expository Writing or Writing in the Sciences didn't match what their students would more likely encounter later in their schooling and careers. Collectively they asked us, "Couldn't you construct a composition course just for majors in medical fields?" We decided we could.

First, however, we would have to investigate what a medical writing course should include. Two of my associates, Jan Lindholm, assistant director of the composition program, and Katherine Guenther, an instructor with a long-standing interest in medical writing, met with curriculum directors in each department that might contribute students. In addition to the majors already mentioned, these included respiratory therapy, medical technology, pharmacy, and mortuary science.

The reports they brought back provided more consternation than anything else. They discovered, for example, that nurses' on-the-job writing mainly involves recording on charts the patients' conditions and treatment. Consequently, "charting" appeared to be a writing activity we should teach. The School of Nursing had other ideas, however. Charting, they told Jan, involves some highly technical details. Not doing it just right could result in a patient's death and a lawsuit for the hospital and the nurse. If we taught it, the nursing faculty would probably have to "unteach" their students and have them learn over. In short, charting must remain a writing skill taught by nurses. (Since then the nursing school has decided to leave charting to two-year degree LPNs and to increase its emphasis on professional writing with students seeking the four-year BSN degree).

Compared to dentists, nurses could still learn much from their composition instructors. Dentists, we were told, "don't write anything." They hire receptionists and secretaries to handle the limited writing involved in running a small business. Even patient charts are virtually void of writing. One dental school faculty member told me: "They've got it down now to where they just pull out a drawing of the dentition and mark an X next to the problem tooth and another X next to a multiple-choice description of the possible problems. They hand that to a dental assistant or a secretary, and she takes care of any records." What were we going to teach predental students to write? More importantly, *why* were we going to teach predental students to write? And what were we going to do with them in a course filled with nurses-, doctors-, and morticians-to-be?

We stopped worrying so much when Jan and Kate noted that every department had mentioned ethics as something they wanted taught in the Writing in the Health Sciences course. This surprised us. We hadn't even thought to ask if biomedical ethics were something we should cover. Indeed, our first reaction on hearing their request was to say that we really weren't prepared to teach ethics. After all, it seemed to us that if the health sciences departments wanted someone to teach their students biomedical ethics, they would do far better by contacting the university's own Biomedical Ethics Center, whose director, Arthur Caplan, is renowned and interviewed worldwide as a leading authority in this area. No, they responded, we don't have time to discuss ethics in our classes. We've got too much material we have to cover. Besides, we think ethics is best taught by instructors in the humanities. Health science students need to think and write about biomedical ethics. What better place to do so than a composition course for health science majors?

What better place indeed. Our call to the Biomedical Ethics Center provided us with some guidance. A few miles away in St. Paul, Greenhaven Press published a book titled *Biomedical Ethics,* a volume in its "Opposing Viewpoints" series. Its articles contained not only good, cross-disciplinary readings but provided a rhetorical model to guide students in their own writings on ethics. Another book the Center recommended was *Cases in Bioethics: Selections from the Hastings Center Report.* In addition, Kate, now designated to teach the first section, began collecting other materials, attempting to gain a sense of the range of writing about medicine. These included everything from back issues of the *Journal of the American Medical Association* and the *Harvard Medical School Health Letter* to Dr. Lewis Thomas' *Lives of a Cell* and Norman Cousin's *Anatomy of an Illness*.

A problem arose. To our horror, Kate's endeavors soon slowed then stopped. She had contracted multiple sclerosis. Her lengthy (and successful) recovery in the hospital gave her ironic pause and a first-hand opportunity to ask medical personnel about their writing. In the months ahead, the research she conducted from her hospital bed provided grist for health science writing anecdotes, which I relayed to the sections of the new Writing in the Health Sciences I would now be teaching. Indeed, as soon as word of Kate's hospitalization arrived in our office, Chris Anson, our director, asked me if I would pick up where Kate had left off by completing the syllabus and teaching the prototype health science writing section. I immediately decided to adapt the "publication approach" I had designed for first-year students the previous quarter to the new course for juniors and seniors.

The publication approach, now standard fare in many composition classes at Minnesota, owes much to the pedagogy of Brazilian educator Paulo Freire. Through it, students invent their own themes, around which they publish their own magazines. Inspired by Stephen Tchudi's theme-centered courses at Michigan State University, a workshop using the publication approach goes beyond a compilation of students'. work in anthologies. Instead, every class contains four to five editorial boards, which solicit articles from class members. The boards work in dynamic tension with conventional peer conferencing groups. When one of its members receives a rejection slip or editorial advice from a board to which she has submitted an article, each conference group acts as a writing support group. Moreover, since each class member belongs to one board and one conference group, each article submitted is read and responded to by eight to ten persons. The publication approach provides several pedagogical advantages. Most importantly, it takes students through a collaborative process that ends with a tangible product of their own creation. The pride they take in their product instills unmatched motivation. It reestablishes students as topic inventors, a role teachers usurped from up-and-coming writers at the beginning of the twentieth century. Indeed, a teacher using this approach slips easily into the role of mentor, coaching students as they decide what to insert in their magazines and how. In addition, a publication approach builds on the power of play. It taps students' collective knowledge and skill as they work together in producing a magazine that resembles those on sale at newsstands.

The publication approach had proven a rich success with first-year students. A few modifications gave it even more success with students at the upper-division. The first and most apparent change I made was, not surprisingly, the course readings. In addition to Green-haven's *Biomedical Ethics*, which included pro and con arguments on artificial insemination, surrogate parenting, genetic engineering, and animal experimentation, students read from a coursepack containing as broad a range of writing about medicine as I could find. In addition to the standard models of medical writing that one might expect—research articles from the *Journal of the American Medical Association*, for example, and an issue of the *Berkeley Wellness Letter*—I inserted Norman Cousin's chapter "Anatomy of an Illness as Perceived by the Patient." Some selections from Lewis Thomas' *The Medusa and the Snail* included "Medical Lessons from History" and "On Natural Death." Dr. Richard Selzer's narrative "Sarcophagus," recounting the loss of one of his cancer patients in the operating room, also appeared on the reading list. I even included two poems: "The Wound-Dresser," written by Walt Whitman when he served as a nurse tending soldiers in the Civil War, and "Labor Pains," Japanese poet Yosano Akiko's lexical image of the emotions present at birth. Two parodies of medical writing also gained entry to the coursepack, thanks to Kate's copy of *The Journal of Irreproducible Results*. The value of the parodies proved itself when, on the day of discussion, it became apparent that more than half the students believed the parodies reported real research. Their discovery that they did not allowed us to explore how the authors employed the conventions of biomedical rhetoric while telling what amounted to a big joke. Among other things, the readings provided the students with prompts for their journal writing. Many entries revealed the students' reflections on the ideas they were reading. Taken together, the readings also permitted the view of how writing in the health sciences varied, sometimes drastically, depending on the audience for whom and the purpose for which it was written.

For the same reason, I modified the syllabus requirements regarding writing assignments. The first change was to specify the audience types and purposes for which the articles would be written. Even though a central principle of the publication approach is that students select their own topics, a teacher can still direct students to give them practice with certain genres and registers. In the case of health-science writers, I recognized that students needed practice addressing both popular and professional audiences. Although undergraduates in the health sciences have been enrolled in only a year or two of majors courses, they enjoy trying on the linguistic clothes of their chosen field, with its specialized lexicon and linguistic conventions. In short, they enjoy sounding like what they think their professors sound like. Many, when they write on a topic in their field, attempt to put on all the clothes in their disciplinary closet, their essays sounding more like a page out of the *Merck Manual* than a professor in class. The same holds true whether they address fellow health professionals or a group of patients. The sociolinguistic prestige and sophistication that accompanies medical jargon proves all too attractive to many health science majors and difficult to put aside. (Indeed, the same holds true for physicians, as my colleague Jim Kaufmann discovered during his dissertation research on the rhetoric of medical writing.) My remedy was to require that at least one article by each student address an audience of patients or others not trained in the health sciences. Another article had to be aimed at professionals in the student's field. Indeed, students could write about the same topic to each audience so that they might more directly see the contrast in each readership's demands. Most chose different topics, as much for variety as anything else. The few who did choose the same topic usually did so thinking they would save themselves extra work. They discovered rather quickly that adjusting their writing to a different set of readers was a more difficult and demanding task than they had imagined.

A second change from the first-year syllabus was the stipulation that a third article take a stand on a medical issue. This requirement stemmed from the requests by the health sciences departments that students write about biomedical ethics. My hope was that the students would follow-up on discussions of the arguments in the "Opposing Viewpoints" book, as well as other readings we covered. To my surprise, most of them avoided the topics we discussed and chose their own instead. To my delight, these tended to grow out of their own experiences, moving readers with their powerful personal insight.

The most memorable and instructive example of this occurred with a class about a year after the new course began. During a discussion of ethics, and before the students had decided firmly on all their paper topics, one of the class members, who was a nurse's aide, mentioned the difficulty of treating Jehovah's Witnesses when they refused blood transfusions. As she ended, an immigrant African student seated right next to her softly intoned, "I'm a Jehovah's Witness." As all the students whirled around to listen, she gently explained the Levitical injunction against draining the blood of an animal and the Witnesses' application of the verse to human blood transfusions. She also described some of the alternative treatments that Witnesses accepted. After the initial shock, the nurse's aide excitedly asked her neighbor about books she could recommend on alternative treatments. The two met frequently to consult each other on their thoughtful, complementary articles, which appeared side-by-side in the same magazine. The nurse's aide examined several situations in which medical personnel must take into account a patient's religious beliefs, a large part of which was devoted to treating Jehovah's Witnesses. The other student's article dealt specifically with blood transfusions and Jehovah's Witnesses. The process these two students went through, as well as the final products they composed, allowed everyone in the class to prepare for scenarios they might encounter in their health science careers. It also allowed them to learn about and appreciate differences between religious beliefs and medical culture, as well as the differences between African and North American cultures.

Writing in the Health Sciences students have produced several dozen magazines, some of whose titles include *Public Health in a Changing Society, The Minnesota Journal of Birth and Genetics, AIDSline, Pediatrics, Dentally Speaking, Nutritional News, Emergency Care and You,* and *Fine Line: A Journal of Transplant and Trauma.* Not all or even most of the articles within these publications address biomedical ethics, of course, although a sizable number do. Occasionally a class decides to devote an entire magazine to ethics. For instance, the articles about blood transfusions appeared in *The Journal of Ethical Dilemma in Health Care,* an issue that also contained such articles as "Surrogacy: Banning Is Not the Answer," "Infanticide: History and Imperiled Newborns," "The Ethics of Recipient Selection in Organ Transplantation," and "Our Elderly: Treatment of the Elderly in the U.S. vs. Cambodia" (authored by a Cambodian resettled in St. Paul).

One of the most exciting episodes in teaching the course came when one student's writing was put to practical use. Patty Ahart, a junior and a nursing major in the very first section I taught of the course, announced within the first few weeks that she wanted to write an article on babies born addicted to cocaine. To support her way through school, Patty was working as a nurse's aide at the university hospital. She had recently witnessed the birth of a cocaine baby and was distressed at the inevitable prospect of more addicted mothers giving birth to addicted infants. The phenomenon was so new to the Twin Cities, however, that she had trouble finding local authorities on the subject or even published medical articles. When she was nearly ready to give up and try another topic, she discovered a physician in town who had just returned from a medical conference in Los Angeles focusing on cocaine births. The doctor was kind enough to give Patty copies of all the information she had brought back, as well as to talk with her at length about what she had learned. Before long, Patty wrote a highly engaging piece warning the Twin Cities' hospital employees of the problems encountered in Los Angeles and suggesting what to do when they cropped up in Minnesota.

Within a few months the number of cocaine babies was indeed increasing in Minneapolis and St. Paul. Patty found herself describing to her co-workers at the university hospital what she had discovered while researching her paper for Writing for the Health Sciences. The nurses on her ward began asking for copies of her article. Soon Patty's supervisor found out about it and asked for permission to print her piece in brochure form, to be passed out to health care workers coming onto the ward. As a result, Patty's article became the first Minnesota piece on cocaine babies distributed among health care workers in the state.

Writing for the Health Sciences has run successfully for over three years in the form I have described. Learning about the health sciences by writing in, for, and about them seems to be a natural. In particular, writing about biomedical ethics is an especially appropriate way to formulate an understanding of the issues swirling through the health sciences. Come to think of it, English and biology are not so separate after all.

Note

Guides to the publication approach to teaching writing are available for both instructors and students at cost. Send requests to Bruce Maylath, Program in Composition and Communication, 306 Lind Hall, University of Minnesota, 207 Church St. SE, Minneapolis, MN 55455.

References

Bach, J. S., ed. 1987. *Biomedical Ethics.* Opposing Viewpoints Series. St. Paul, MN: Greenhaven Press.

Britton, J. 1970. *Language and Learning.* Harmondsworth, England: Penguin.

Freire, P. 1970. *Pedagogy of the Oppressed.* New York: Seabury Press.

Kaufmann, J. M. 1988. "The Rhetoric of Medical Writing: Case Studies of Physicians Writing for Journal Publication." Diss. University of Minnesota.

Levine, C. 1989. *Cases in Bioethics: Selections from the Hastings Center Report.* New York: St. Martin's Press.

Moffett, J. 1968. *Teaching the Universe of Discourse.* Boston: Houghton Mifflin.

Tchudi, S. N. 1986. *Teaching Writing in the Content Areas—College Level.* Washington, D.C.: National Education Association.

13 Understanding Technological Risk through Literature

Judith Laurence Pastore
University of Massachusetts at Lowell

. . . the intellectual separation of the 'two cultures' is said to be a problem of our time, but this separation is inevitable, it is going steadily to increase, not decrease, and it cannot possibly be cured by having humanists read more popular science or scientists read more poetry. The real problem is not the humanist's ignorance of science or vice versa, but the ignorance of both humanist and scientist about the society of which they are both citizens. The quality of an intellectual's social imagination is the quality of his maturity as a thinker, whatever his brilliance in his own line.

Northrop Frye, *Varieties of Literary Utopias.*

The difficulty many people encounter in understanding technological risk can often be traced to the way they have been educated. Instead of combining instruction about how technical projects are designed and constructed with analysis of how technology affects society, most U.S. education artificially compartmentalizes learning, with the result that students rarely get "the big picture." If we hope to prepare future generations to meet the challenge technological risk presents in almost every area of modern existence, we may have to jettison many of the abstract instructional approaches currently used and substitute interdisciplinary teaching that combines vocational theory and training with a broad range of humanistic studies, including analysis of language and literature. For many preoccupied with the specifics of particular disciplines, such an approach is viewed not merely as heretical, but downright nonsensical. After all, what have poetry and novels to do with building better bridges and missiles? But if educators hope to prepare students to make responsible evaluations in a realistic social context, they need to rethink the rationale of our current educational structure. In one sense we need to take some educational risks to be able to understand technological risk, because if winning a war is too important to leave to generals, then understanding and controlling modern technology is too important to trust to individual disciplines.

Understanding Technological Risk, the team-taught, interdisciplinary course discussed here, uses three literary texts to focus on a set of scientific problems: new experiments, the development of atomic energy, and toxic accidents. But the same approach could be applied to any number of interdisciplinary topics, including environmental pollution, energy, population explosion, world health, or AIDS. The aim of the course is to make students realize that future problem solving will involve a combination of specific vocational training with an understanding of the limitations of such training and an awareness that they must learn much more from a variety of fields before they can hope to make intelligent decisions.

Our course evolved as a result of a three-year grant from the National Endowment for the Humanities in 1978 to fund team-teaching on technology and values by scientists and humanists. The courses developed in the program continued after the grant ran out. I participated in the introductory course for a number of years before Gilbert Brown, a nuclear engineer, decided he wanted to become involved. Although most people teaching the course focused on their area of expertise, Gil was reluctant to talk about nuclear issues, particularly when so many people had negative attitudes about it. Similarly, I was reluctant to focus on language and literature, particularly since the course was classified not as a humanities offering, but as one of the social science electives students could take to fulfill their general education requirements. So as strange creations sometimes become officially entrenched in academia, a nuclear engineer and a humanist ended up teaching a social science course, with both of us, though thoroughly committed to the course's ideology, repressing our natural interests.

Our first breakthrough came when Gil became intrigued by risk theory as a way of responding to the nuclear debate and suggested we use William Lowrance's excellent text on the subject, *Of Appropriate Risk*. Still reluctant to introduce his own concerns about nuclear power, he nevertheless found an opportunity to examine with the students one of the cogent arguments about nuclear safety. Unfortunately, the book went out of print the following year. We next tried a collection called *Readings in Risk*, which also contained excellent material, but had so many different topics and viewpoints that the students ultimately felt overwhelmed. The next year we used H. W. Lewis's *Technological Risk* with greater success because, like the pattern of our course, he approaches the topic from an interdisciplinary point of view, frequently explaining technical concepts with literary analogies.

But the real turning point came one evening in 1988 at a Guthrie Theater production, when separately with our respective spouses, we viewed Barbara Field's highly innovative dramatic interpretation of the Frankenstein myth. Meeting during intermission, Gil said: "Hey. This is great. We should be teaching the novel." One month later, after reading Richard Rhodes' *The Making of the Atomic Bomb,* I found myself echoing him: "Gil. This is great. We should be teaching it." Thus we gave each other permission to do what each of us had been repressing, and from that point the course really took off. We had already discovered Don DeLillo's satiric novel *White Noise* (1984), about a dangerous chemical accident, written after Three Mile Island but before Bhopal and Chernobyl. So with that, *Frankenstein,* Rhodes, and at that time Lowrance as our texts, we gradually evolved a format that permitted us to work in the many related themes we wanted to explore. Nevertheless, we realized that our particular bead on the "two cultures" controversy could go off target if either of us seemed to be proselytizing for our area of specialization. We got around this by being as open as we could about our interests and biases. Naturally, there were always a few students who resented having to read novels in anything but an English course and those who thought anyone advocating nuclear energy was a minister of Satan. But by openly admitting what our predilections were, we hoped to preclude any sense that either of us had an insidious hidden agenda.

Our other problem came from our mutual desire to make students aware of how much language use affects how they think. We knew we could make the course writing intensive, but that was no guarantee that students would accept the importance of language analysis. Although many modern philosophers and social analysts, including Wittgenstein, Derrida, and Foucault, stress how much language molds how we perceive reality, the structure of university education usually limits analysis of language to mastering the terminology of the chosen field. Moreover, analysis of language generally is held to be the purview of English courses, which most students take only when required, seldom learning that it is the language of a culture that largely determines and reflects the culture's values.

To overcome this problem we decided to reclassify the course as an upper-level humanities offering, rechristened "Understanding

Technological Risk." We were then free to focus on the ways different types of literature approach questions of safety, benefits, and potential dangers involved in technological decisions.

We begin the course with Mary Shelley's 1818 novel *Frankenstein*, which offers a wealth of themes for any course concerned with technological risk. The most familiar theme, of course, is that science and technology practiced in isolation can create monsters capable of destroying not only their creators but society itself. Many students begin the novel favoring Dr. Frankenstein and prejudiced against the Creature. Their response tended to reverse when they read the Creature's narrative. For example, during one discussion, Ed, a math major, compared him to Grendel in *Beowulf,* saying: "They were both ostracized because they were ugly. It really wasn't their fault." Tim, an engineering student, however, replied: "That doesn't justify the Creature's killing William and planting the locket on Justine. Neither of them ever did anything to him." Lisa, a business major, was angry with Dr. Frankenstein for not coming forward: "He's the only one who knows it was the Creature and not Justine who committed the crime. How can he stand by and let her be hung for a crime she didn't do?" It became clear to the class as the discussion progressed that simplistic either/or interpretations of the novel belie its many complexities. Although generally sympathetic to the Creature, the class as a whole would not absolve him of guilt, nor would they wholly condemn Frankenstein's attempt to create life from disparate body parts. "If he had been a better workman and taken more time to make the Creature beautiful," Sean, another engineering student, argued, "perhaps he and the Creature would have become friends, and Frankenstein could have taught him how to be a good person." The class agreed that viewing technology as either inherently good or inherently evil—Caliban or Ariel, as I the English teacher phrase it— misses the point. They further agreed that for better or worse, technology is not going to go away; it has become embedded into almost every area of our lives. Frankenstein came to symbolize bad science for them, not necessarily because he violates any "natural law" of human reproduction (although some students also insisted that he had), but because he had taken too many risks to achieve his goal without also taking the necessary precautions to maximize safety. Tim, a civil engineering major, concluded: "He should have first done a thorough environmental impact study."

As the discussion for this section wrapped up, students began to recognize that viewing science and technology as creators of either

Armaggedon or Paradise employs an outmoded thinking pattern, one that views the workings of science as abstract entities rather than as existentially interactive. To encourage them to question such a simplistic approach further, we asked them to write an essay pinpointing the mistakes Victor Frankenstein had made, and how they would have behaved differently. Another time we asked them to analyze the monster's nature for both good and evil traits. A third time, we asked them to imagine themselves at a crucial moment in their chosen field faced with a decision that pitted their personal ambition against the social good. All of these assignments have proven successful in enabling students to see the novel as more than simply an old-fashioned horror story.

Another method we use to help them appreciate the complexity of Shelley's language is to show the famous 1931 film version that introduced Boris Karloff. Some of the visuals echo the themes of the novel in a surprisingly sophisticated manner—the use of fire throughout for example, a technology that is neither good nor evil, in essence, but can go either way if used improperly. In many other ways, the film's naive plot and characterization encourage most students to see how much more the novel accomplishes—no mean feat in the television age. On the evaluations that we ask students to complete at the end of the semester, many of them suggest dropping the film, saying "The book is much better. I never realized how much it differs from the movie."

Another assignment we used one year based on *Frankenstein* asked students to question whether technological risks depicted in the novel might also occur in their chosen fields. Several chemical engineering students found strong connections: Daphne Holmes made the following comparison[1]:

> In the book, Frankenstein was driven by some inner force to create a living organism out of non-living material. He was so into his work that he looked at himself as God and said, "A new species would bless me as its creator and source; many happy and excellent natures would owe their being to me" (39). He didn't at any point stop to think of the implications it would have on the rest of the world. In Chemical Engineering you can't think of yourself as superior to everyone else because you aren't. Many mistakes can be made if you don't stop to think what would happen if you put two chemicals together at wrong pressures or temperatures. You have to think ahead of how to transport chemicals safely, and if there is some accident in which the chemical leaks, you have to think of a fast efficient way to

clean it up. There are almost always unwanted chemicals made in a process which you have to dispose. In this case you have to think of ways of disposing of them without hurting the environment or the people in it.

Kurt Schmidt, also a chemical engineering major, was very concerned with problems of pollution and felt that if he ever were to contribute, even inadvertently, to the greenhouse effect or "smog problems in large cities," "I would feel as Frankenstein did when he created the monster: 'Oh! No mortal could support the horror . . .'" (57). Ian MacCarthy, a business major, felt that the novel raised many ethical questions appropriate to his field: "Related to my field of business are issues like: determinism vs. free will; is being too ambitious bad; and discrimination."

John Russo, an electrical engineering major, compared Frankenstein's work to the use of industrial robots.

> Suppose an electrical engineer discovers a way to make an industrial robot perform a task better, faster, and cheaper than a worker can. . . . This robot could put thousands of people out of work, drastically changing their lives.

John then examined some of the possible social ramifications of this particular engineering application, concluding that "the electrical engineering profession, as well as any engineering profession, has value issues associated with it which appear in *Frankenstein*."

Gary O'Hara, another electrical engineering major, considered how the monster paralleled developments in artificial intelligence (AI):

> At the beginning of the novel, the monster is very much like the computers of today. A lifeless hunk of matter that can do absolutely nothing. Then, after Frankenstein instilled life in his creation, it was analogous to "hitting the power switch." Suddenly, his creation worked, and could perform tasks.
>
> This is where AI comes into play. A computer, once turned on, must be given a set of commands, usually supplied by an operator or programmer. This person can exhibit "god-like" control over the computer. . . . Frankenstein had no control over his creation. The creature moved, thought, rationalized, reasoned, and learned. This is what AI aims to do.

Gary concluded by emphasizing the need to do thorough risk analysis, stating that those working on AI have to take "all proper precautions . . . so that today's society does not create (or recreate) Frankenstein's monster."

Finally, Bill Flaherty, another electrical engineering student, analyzed the multiple effects on family and society produced by Frankenstein's risky experiment. He believes engineers today can also use applied technology "poorly or irresponsibly."

> Towards the end of the book, Frankenstein realizes, as he is building the monster a mate, that he does have a responsibility to society, and that he cannot create another monster in good conscience. This is why he "tore to pieces" and aborted his monster's mate before she was completed.

Understanding technological risk also requires some awareness of how science has been viewed over the centuries. We discuss Thomas Kuhn's metaphor of science as a series of major paradigm shifts in how different ages and cultures have interpreted the operations of the physical world. "I thought metaphors were something poets used," Tom commented one year. "How can something fictional be valid in explaining science?" "Are black holes, quasars, and quarks any more scientific?" I replied. "Aren't they metaphors for physical realities we cannot see with the naked eye and have to accept the existence of on faith?" We discuss the human tendency to create images to explain abstract concepts: Santa Claus, Uncle Sam, God. We also consider how cognition creates abstract theories or fictions to explain the complex workings of the universe: the Ptolemaic theory, evolution, the Big Bang. This encourages students to think about how new technologies impact not only the material world but the metaphysical—the ideas we formulate, the concepts we use to define what we envision as reality. This discussion provides a segue to the discovery of atomic energy—the most notable paradigm shift of this half of the twentieth century. We discuss how the transition from Newtonian to quantum physics occurred at a particularly auspicious time for the rapid dissemination of information, and how open access to earlier knowledge speeds up the process of making new discoveries, which has been true from the breakthroughs of the Copernican revolution to the early world of computer hackers. In the early days of nuclear discoveries, before World War II, an era that Richard Rhodes christens a "Republic of Science" existed among international physicists, facilitating rapid advances in knowledge. The early chapters in Rhodes's *The Making of the Atomic Bomb* depict this world, so we concentrate on the first half of the text. Although we strongly urge students also to read the second half, we do not require it, since the book is 788 pages, much of it highly factual and/or technical. As a substitute, we show the documentary about the rise and fall of J. Robert Oppenheimer, *The Day After Trinity*.

Over the years, we have used a number of different writing assignments in this portion of the course. Once, to show how difficult objective assessment of historical data can be, we asked them to imagine that it is August 7, 1945, and they have just learned that an atomic bomb has been dropped the day before on Hiroshima. They learn that President Truman plans to drop a second bomb. We asked them to write a letter to the President arguing for or against the second atomic attack, urging them to take a stand and, if they could not, to explain their ambivalence as clearly as they could. We also discussed the differences between logical argument and emotional persuasion, and how the former should ultimately produce greater conviction. To illustrate the value of using primary sources, we handed out an article dated August 10, 1945, from the periodical *Engineering,* featuring an account of the blast at Hiroshima accompanied by an official statement from Winston Churchill, but making no mention of the second blast.

Another writing assignment we have used asked students to employ what they have learned thus far about technology, values, and understanding risk to contrast the scientific decisions made by Frankenstein with those made by J. Robert Oppenheimer. Yet another asked them to create an imaginary scenario in which they have finally achieved their career goals and are confronted with a technological problem requiring a personal evaluation of the risks, benefits, and values. How would they go about making their decision?

Finally, we worked out an assignment to draw on earlier discussions of *Frankenstein* and the temptation to reduce complex issues to simplistic either/or scenarios. The assignment was to take one of the three theories mentioned in Rhodes—Einstein's relativity, Bohr's complementarity, or Heisenberg's uncertainty—and to discuss whether or not the following conflicting statements could be resolved:

> Some say the development of the atomic bomb was inherently evil.
> Some say the development of the atomic bomb was an inevitable step in society's ongoing quest for knowledge.

Most of the students went to outside sources to learn more about the theory they chose. In some cases, their understanding still remained faulty or reductive—"Heisenberg's theory proves you can never know anything"; "Einstein's relativity theory means nothing is ever right or wrong." Overall, though, their essays demonstrated an ability to integrate a complex theoretical framework with a practical values question.

This ability was further tested in the final segment of the course with discussion of the novel *White Noise*, written by the postmodern American satirist Don DeLillo who analyzes in all his work the impact of technology on American culture. Published in 1984, *White Noise* dramatizes a lethal chemical accident in a quiet college community. By studying technological risk in a literary context quite different from the gothic/science fiction world of *Frankenstein*, or the historical world of Rhodes, students see how varying literary techniques can get at realms of existence closed to the linear, Cartesian method.

DeLillo's style is also very useful in a course designed to show students the synthesizing role of language, since language, rather than plot or characterization, is his principal interest. Before I taught *White Noise*, I worried that its sophisticated postmodern humor would escape undergraduates. But I underestimated our students. The majority end up loving its zany dialogue.

In the second part of the novel, the central characters, the Gladney family, must evacuate their home because of a freak chemical accident. A freight car carrying the deadly chemical Nyodene D is rammed by an adjacent car whose coupling pierces it, creating a leak that the radio at first calls "a feathery plume" (111), then a "black billowing cloud," and finally the "airbourne toxic event." This innocuous "state-created terminology" (117) contrasts throughout with the nightmarish scenes DeLillo describes. The contrast brings home to students how linguistic mediations are employed to distort our comprehension of reality. The father, Jack Gladney, inadvertently becomes exposed to the deadly substance when he leaves his car for two minutes to get gasoline. The remainder of the novel deals with how he and his wife cope with their ever-growing fear of death.

The final assignment in the course asks students to write on one aspect of technology in *White Noise* and answer these questions:

1. How does DeLillo present this technology? Show this by including a number of relevant passages from the novel, expressed in your own words.

2. What is DeLillo's attitude towards this technology based on what you understand about the rest of *White Noise*? Again paraphrase relevant passages.

3. From what you know, how accurately does DeLillo depict this technology and its effects? Cite sources of your information, such as other courses, work or personal experience, relevant authorities, scholarly journals, newspapers, or periodical articles.

4. Based on your understanding of H. W. Lewis' *Technological Risk*, how accurately does DeLillo depict the risks this technology poses?

5. What is your attitude toward this technology and why?

Tom, a senior electrical engineering major, wrote about the breakdown in authority that occurs throughout the novel, and how that puts the welfare of many at risk. He also discussed how "the comforts created by modern technology that we now take for granted have left us feeling an undeserved sense of invincibility as a class."

> Reinforcing this sense of invincibility and spawning a host of other social problems is the omnipresent mass media, particularly television. It has the power to make one famous and to legitimize actions in the eyes of the viewer. Heinrich's chess partner killed people to become immortal . . . . The nightly parade of tragedies and disasters have weaned people of any compassion for victims. We look for quality disasters, bread and circus . . . . The Gladney's set is always on in some room of the house . . . . When a family constantly exposes itself at whatever level to television, they risk losing touch with each other.

Gerald Quirk, a biology major interested in genetic research, analyzed how the microorganisms released to destroy the toxic cloud could in turn create greater technological risks.

> Like all technologies, genetic engineering, or recombinant DNA, has its own set of risks and benefits. This is one of the technologies DeLillo accurately portrays. In *White Noise*, the benefit is obvious: the microorganisms clean up the cloud preventing further damage and an end to the airborne toxic event. The risks, however are understated and can be divided into two sections.

Gerald proceeds to explain first how the public gets a misperception of genetic engineering risks from "supermarket tabloids such as *The National Enquirer* or *Star,*" which DeLillo refers to a number of times in the novel. Because these publications treat this technology as sensational science fiction, "people will fear it instead of respecting it": "The more limited the knowledge, the greater the fear." The second risk Gerald mentions comes from the scientists themselves. Here, he quotes Babette Gladney: "What scares me is have they [the scientists] thought it through completely" (161). He goes on to point out that no amount of laboratory testing can ever totally "simulate real world conditions." Winnie Richards, a neurochemist at the college where Jack teaches, questions if the spectacular sunsets they now have are a residue from the microorganisms. Gerald then quotes Lewis's statement in *Technological Risk* that we must remain uncertain "when our needs exceed the state of knowledge about a subject" (102). Before genetic engineering can proceed with assurances of maximum safety to the public, many ethical issues must first be addressed:

> Scientists can already clone skin, could a person be next? Who, as we take command of genes, gets to play God? Can we actually expect to improve on Mother Nature's job or does she indeed know best? Who will set the goals for genetic engineering? Does man have the right to infringe on such a delicate balance in nature that has been running efficiently for eons? Will genetic engineering grant more freedoms or become a way of enslaving? Is genetic engineering worth the risks?

Writing has worked in this course because the essay assignments combine a specific theoretical orientation that focuses on technological risk with a variety of literary viewpoints. But each essay is also designed to elicit creative personal responses from the students who frequently turn in highly imaginative work. Many of them comment that, unlike most writing they have had to do in college, they have actually enjoyed doing these assignments. We believe that a similar interdisciplinary approach can be employed using literature to illustrate numerous scientific topics. What is important is to break out of the older compartmentalized mode that is smothering the vitality of American education and to experiment with creative projects that will stimulate young minds.

Note

1. Pseudonyms are used when quoting student comments and papers. Instead of using the pedantic [*sic*], I have corrected simple grammatical and spelling errors, but have generally let the students' language stand.

References

DeLillo, D. 1986. *White Noise*. New York: Penguin.

Glickman, T. S., and M. Gough, eds. 1990. *Readings in Risk*. Washington, D.C.: Resources for the Future.

Lewis, H. W. 1991. *Technological Risk*. New York: W.W. Norton.

Lowrance, W. W. 1976. *Of Acceptable Risk: Science and the Determination of Safety*. Los Altos, Calif., William Kaufmann.

Rhodes, R. 1988. *The Making of the Atomic Bomb.* New York: Simon & Schuster/Touchstone Paperback.

Shelley, M. 1981. *Frankenstein.* New York: Bantam.

Epilogue:
Dry Bones

Mike Pope
Virginia State University

A colleague of mine keeps a file of the essays he wrote as a college freshman on his desk. I understand, because I know that somewhere in my attic hides one of my freshman themes in which there's a now obvious confusion of the terms *integration* and *segregation,* as most people use those words. No wonder that one main memory of my English teacher is this caring woman turning to the class at least once a week, asking, "Can't you wiggle one little brain cell?" She knew that learners' ideas are not gift-wrapped packages from caring teachers or from earlier times, but something that comes from "wiggling" brain cells.

My teacher must have believed that students understand through constructs that they create with language. The teachers who have written for the book you are reading have constructed accounts from their experiences with learners. They have discussed students' thinking about the world in ways similar to their own and in other ways: through exploration, discovery, insight. When we read about their world or observe ours, we create. We are thinking our own thoughts, with the symbols and patterns suggested by others. One reader may not use symbols and patterns exactly as the writer uses them, but the similarity of their ideas depends on the extent that the images, symbols, and patterns that the reader generates—from experiences—are like the writer's.

If meanings were gifts that could be transported through letters or sounds to learners, the teacher's job would be simply to present written materials and talk; but talking, like writing, is a composing-structuring-learning act. Meanings are not communicable; whether a reader or writer, one's ideas come from his or her own synthesis (Pope 1989). For example, if I were to say that "an enzyme reads messenger-RNA," the degree that an observer's meaning would be like mine will be the degree that the observer's language patterns and memories coincide with mine, learned and remembered from experiences using

English and playing geneticist. Meanings, therefore, come from what one has made of experiences and the structures formed from them. Although students have not accumulated a teacher's experience, they are often expected to develop meanings like those of the teacher, to see what the teacher sees, to learn what might be called the teacher's subject.

Texts are gifts, but not of ideas and understandings. They are representations of the writer's symbols and patterns of ideas, which remain with the author. When observers become interested in what another has done and said, they can create symbol systems like that of the person whose actions and utterances they observe, and can construct ideas similar to that person's. To develop interrelated ideas like those of another, to learn that person's subject, the initiate must do what the expert has done.

Ideally, learners become apprentices to experts, watching what they do, listening to what they say as they perform, and acting like them. If the experts are concerned mainly with abstract matters, and their performance is restricted to the manipulating of symbols, the learners will be similarly concerned and will manipulate symbols likewise, imaging the referents of those symbols as they perform. Of course, one of the teacher's responsibilities is to promote that imagination. Teaching a subject means getting learners to think about the world as experienced composers. The learner, as Ann E. Berthoff puts it, makes the meaning (1983). The teacher can ask learners to think about matters that he or she deems important and can guide the making.

It appears that humans are aware of much, much more than they are conscious of. Robert Pirsig in *Zen and the Art of Motorcycle Maintenance* likens what we are conscious of to a handful of sand selected from an "endless landscape of awareness" (1980). He believes that the selecting into consciousness changes that little bit of awareness, and the result is what the individual calls the world (1980, 69). Then, to understand the world, the learner divides it, distinguishing one piece from another. The learner's distinctions are structures that are formed, not because the world is being divided, but through distinctions in the person's consciousness, as the learner labels and relates that which first appears to be uniform. Hereabout—where experiences are brought into consciousness and the learner can make something of them—lives the problem of teachers who care about the meanings that their students make, the subjects that they compose.

Telling, by the teacher, can be a beginning for a student (if most of the teacher's words are within the student's experiences/syntactic reach), but often students perceive it as an ending, the last word, the "truth" that, as Socrates believed, remains unreal to the learner (if it continues to exist at all). Emerson, in his introduction to *Nature*, warned of the same problem, disparaging those satisfied with the "dry bones" of others (7). Students may not know that the teacher's truth can be unreal (to them) and the bones dry.

Once in an introductory linguistics course, I was attempting to get the students to understand the Greeks' invention of the alphabet. One student said that the Greeks borrowed some letters from the Phoenicians and came up with the alphabet. Noting that the statement was phrased similarly to the text, I asked the person to explain. After a short silence, another student said, "Well, the Phoenicians gave the Greeks some letters and the Greeks used them to invent the alphabet." I wanted to know what that meant. After a silence longer than the last, a third student, obviously frustrated with me, said, "Look, the Greeks didn't have an alphabet; then the Phoenicians came along and the Greeks borrowed their letters and made the alphabet." Oblivious that I was in the same trap as the students, I said, "But the authors said that the Greeks' invention of the alphabet was a discovery of their phonemic system! What does that mean?" I thought the question was fair because we had already studied the chapter on phonemes. Then a very long silence.

Satisfied with a teacher's or an author's words, learners may never suspect that they do not really know; and when teachers concentrate on what is unfamiliar, the students rarely hear words that are true to them. (The reason the words of Emerson or anybody else are the truth and not dry bones to you and me is that we know they are true before we see them; we *recognize* their truth from our memory and beliefs; we wish that *we* had "said that"—and we have.)

Richard Jones, in a fascinating book called *The Dream Poet*, affirms the importance of "truly believing what we know" (1979, 176). Jones, a psychologist, taught his students to recognize the poet in dream experiences and to relate their findings to literary selections, relying on their own words for understanding. Students who depend on others' words may think that they understand, yet they may find it difficult to move beyond a yawning, so-what attitude. Emerson, in his chapter on language, advises learners to "pierce this rotten diction and fasten words again to visible things" if they wish to be "in alliance with truth" (20). Truly believing—gaining an alliance with truth—

probably can come only from composing, from the sense that the observers make themselves not from the words of others (the truth that remains unreal and that Socrates disdained), but from the observations and discoveries that the learners make or affirm with their own words.

What would one need to recognize the truth of another's words, such as those about the Greeks' invention of the alphabet, instead of imitating them, as Helen Keller said, in "monkeylike fashion" (1903)? What could one do to dis-cover a chapter about phonemic systems? Stanley Fish tells us that one can read only what one already knows—that meaning precedes the words (310–15). In recognizing the "harmony" of others' statements, Pirsig says, we infer that they point to what we have seen (1980, 241). With the observer's knowledge of sentence formation and with memories, harmony is supplied by relating the statements of others with the meanings that have been made or are presently being made. The problem, then, of the teacher who cares about what students see, the meanings that they make, resides in suggesting experiences for students to consider and the constructing of assignments that most likely will lead them to structure memories, compose views out of their selections from awareness, views that are useful, believable.

How the experiences are considered in class as well as the manner in which the assignments are made and responded to is another problem and also, of course, the teacher's responsibility. But the learner is the one who has to make the meaning, make sense. Whether teacher or student, one cannot make the other's sense. Making sense, though, takes place within one's metaviews, beliefs, and attitudes, those usually quite solid structures already formed from previous experiences—what Pirsig calls value rigidity, which can make real (truly believed) learning of new facts unlikely (1980, 279–80). A few years ago in another linguistics class, I asked my students to consider whether grammatical statements were dissections of language or simply pointed toward language; that is, whether one could learn Russian by learning to make statements about the structures of its artifacts. After having the students consider their own experiences, I asked one student to write on the board a true statement to the class (the sentence was *It is 25 minutes until 11:00*) and then asked another to talk about the structures in the sentence. It soon became evident that the second task was much harder than the first; other students and the writer also had difficulty analyzing it. I thought it was obvious that knowing grammatical facts and knowing how to make sentences were different kinds of knowledge. One student came to me after class and said, "I can say what you want me to in class, but I am not going to change my mind about this." Subsequent compositions from the class indicated that a frustrating number of the students still confused grammar and language.

Another problem with trying to get others to see what the teacher sees is that many students, in their natural response to figure out what the teacher wants, may see the situation as a trivial, guess-the-answer-on-the-teacher's-mind game, especially if they have not had much practice in writing or thinking systematically about classroom matters.

Composing views, guessing answers, and neatly stacking dry bones are very different acts. Recording the words of others is not a problem, but imitating them—equating them with knowing—is, I agree with Pirsig, a real evil (1980, 172). Words matter, but whose? If students are asked simply to manipulate the teacher's and author's words or respond to them on objective tests, they may never construct a view; but if the students use their own words to think about their experiences, including experiences with words presented by others, understanding becomes a real possibility. But even when teachers succeed in weaning students from imitation, they are still faced with the fact that the students cannot deliberately understand something. One cannot elect understanding. One can choose to work for understanding, invite it, but it comes in a somewhat mysterious manner. For instance, a person may end a course feeling about ready to start it again, and may develop clear concepts about a subject long after the course. Significant seeing often occurs when one's conscious self seems to be working the least. We have heard stories of how Poincaré, for instance, solved problems when his conscious was focusing on something else or when he was asleep. Just recently, biophysicist Laura Levin, in a moment of leisure, figured out how the clam locks itself in, a puzzle that she had studied for years. I know a man who, twice, worked for days on a problem with a sewing machine and then woke up one morning knowing how to fix it. I know another who "repairs" troublesome stereo and television sets while asleep, making notes to himself during wakeful moments. D. T. Suzuki, in *Essays in Zen Buddhism*, points out what he calls a disquieting quality of the intellect: "Though it raises questions enough to disturb the serenity of the mind, it is too frequently unable to give satisfactory answers to them" (1975, 18). I am saying all of this to point out that if writing is a conscious activity and if understandings are the work of the nonconscious self, it may be asking too much of a student to compose in a specified time solutions to problems that "disturb the serenity of the mind."

It is the learner who invites understanding, but the teacher can help prepare for the invitation. Since meaning is made from experience, probably the most important responsibility of the teacher is getting students to consider (talk, write about) experiences and to compose them with care. Robert Pirsig calls caring "quality," which he describes as "a *relationship* between man and his experience" (1980, 338), the creator of facts, which "preselects what data we're going to be conscious of, and it makes this selection in such a way as to best harmonize what we are with what we are becoming" (1980, 280), "a feeling of identification with what one's doing" (1980, 267). Students probably cannot will this feeling, but an attentive teacher can make assignments that may move them toward this special connection with their experience.

To advance the invitation for understanding, someone—the teacher, the student—must raise questions, questions that disturb one's peace of mind, that puzzle. Pirsig suggests that writing down everything about a problem—what we have seen, what we now see, what we understand the puzzle to be, and what we want to understand—not only brings it into focus, but often suggests potential solutions (1980, 93, 100). Although insight may neither be forced nor hurried, often occurring when the mind appears to be at rest, it can come to those who have a caring relationship with their experience and who welcome puzzlement, "the best possible situation" a learner can be in, for the "mind will naturally and freely move toward a solution" (Pirsig 1980, 256–57).

The writers in this book have not *given to us* any insight or answers that we can value. They have reminded us of some things that we can affirm with our language and experience, and they have invited us to think about language and how we and our students may use it to look at our experience and organize what we see. And they have posed some good questions.

A chemistry professor of mine never tired of saying, "Ninety percent of the answer is knowing what the question is." Since one function of language is the creating of a caring relationship with one's experience, could another be the posing-exploring of questions and problems? What kinds of assignments would help students to create a caring relationship with their experience and come to know questions, to become puzzled and to know why? What assignments would help them communicate with the problem solver within and *dis*cover the answers, should they come?

References

Berthoff, A. 1983. *Reclaiming the Imagination*. Upper Montclair, N.J.: Boynton/Cook Publishers.

Emerson, R. W. 1971. *Nature, Addresses, and Lectures*. The Collected Works of Ralph Waldo Emerson, vol. 1. Cambridge, Mass.: The Belknap Press of Harvard University Press.

Fish, S. 1980. *Is There a Text in This Class?* Cambridge, Mass.: Harvard University Press.

Jones, R. 1979. *The Dream Poet*. Cambridge, Mass.: Schenkman Publishing Company.

Keller, H. 1903. *The Story of My Life*. Garden City, N.Y.: Doubleday and Company.

Pirsig, R. 1980. *Zen and the Art of Motorcycle Maintenance*. New York: Bantam Books.

Pope, M. 1989. A Myth: Whose Thoughts You're Having Now. *Teaching & Learning* 4:47–51.

Suzuki, D. 1975. *Essays in Zen Buddhism*. First Series. London: Rider and Company.

Editor

Stephen Tchudi graduated from Hamilton College with a B.A. in chemistry, a field he then threw over because of a blossoming romance with the humanities and literature, which he has now been teaching for three decades. He is presently professor of English at the University of Nevada, Reno, where he developed the graduate program in rhetoric and composition and teaches in several interdisciplinary programs and projects, including UNR's senior or "capstone" seminars, introductory university seminars for freshmen, and PACE, the Program for Adult College Education. He is a past president of NCTE and former editor of *The English Journal.* He assisted Professor Edward Fagan in founding the Assembly on Science and Humanities of NCTE and has served as the assembly's chair and as editor of its newsletter. He is especially pleased to have edited this volume for NCTE and ASH because it has allowed him to integrate some of his own interests in teaching and, in a very real sense, to understand what that now dusty chemistry degree was all about.

Contributors

Dawn Abt-Perkins is a doctoral candidate in English education at the University of Wisconsin–Madison. She teaches reading and writing courses in the summer and supervises student teachers during the academic year. Before becoming a full-time graduate student, she taught high school English and journalism courses for five years.

Brad Blanchette teaches English and social studies at Colchester High School in Vermont. He has taught interdisciplinary courses, including American Humanities and Science and Society, for ten years. He believes in the synergistic potential of interdisciplinary learning.

Terrie Bridgman is a first grade teacher at the Baker Demonstration School of National-Louis University in Evanston, Illinois. Her interest in the integrated curriculum, particularly in the area of math education, was sparked by her collegiate work with the math department at the University. She feels that integrating math in other areas of the curriculum is a natural component of a primary classroom.

Dr. Pamela Sissi Carroll, assistant professor of English education at Florida State University, received her doctorate from Auburn University. With experience as a classroom teacher at the middle and high school levels, she is currently pursuing interests in the ways students construct meaning as readers of literature and as writers. She is particularly interested in multicultural literature for young adults, and its place in the classroom.

Betty Carvellas teaches science at Colchester High School in Vermont, where she also chairs the Science Department. She helped develop the Science and Society curriculum out of unnerving frustration with the compartmentalization of traditional curricula.

Ann Watson Cohn is a first grade teacher at the Baker Demonstration School of National-Louis University in Evanston, Illinois. Ann by trade is a reading specialist but by passion haunts the university math department office. This dichotomy has allowed her to use children's literature extensively in her math curriculum.

Patricia Tefft Cousin is assistant professor at California State University, San Bernardino. She teaches courses in special education and reading. A former storyteller, she is interested in incorporating the notion of story into all facets of her teaching.

Roy F. Fox is associate professor of English Education at the University of Missouri–Columbia, where he directs the Missouri Writing Project. He became more interested in interdisciplinary studies in the early eighties, when he received a grant from the National Endowment for the Humanities to establish a writing and thinking across the curriculum program at Boise State University, where he served as Director of Writing.

Dr. Alejandro Jose Gallard, assistant professor of science education at Florida State University, received his Ph.D. from Michigan State University. He has taught linguistically diverse inner-city students at the elementary, middle, and high school levels, and has worked extensively with Latin American universities in improving their science education programs. Dr. Gallard is currently interested in classroom and policy issues that pertain to nonnative speakers of English in and beyond the United States.

Karen Gallas teaches first and second grades at the Lawrence School in Brookline, Massachusetts. She is also a member of the Brookline Teacher Research Seminar, and has been conducting research on children's talk since 1988. Her interest in interdisciplinary teaching and learning stems from her longstanding work with the creative arts and learning, but it has been broadened through the process of teacher research.

David Goodney is professor and chair of the Chemistry Department of Willamette University. In addition to traditional chemistry courses, David has team taught interdisciplinary courses such as Science and Society and Chemistry, Economics and the Environment. Along with coauthor Carol Long, he has twice taught the Literature of Natural Science seminar, which provided the material for the essay in this volume.

Erica Jacobs is an English teacher at Thomas Jefferson High School of Science and Technology in Alexandria, Virginia, and a lecturer in writing at George Mason University in Fairfax, Virginia. She became involved with George Mason's Writing Across the Curriculum program in 1980 and has been teaching interdisciplinary courses at Thomas Jefferson.

Carol S. Long has taught in the Department of English at Willamette University in Salem, Oregon, since 1972. Her primary interests are in twentieth-century literature. She teaches courses in the Literature of Natural Science as well as Writing and Science and finds the boundary between scientific and humanistic language an engaging territory.

Mary Maguire is associate professor in the Department of Education in Second Languages at McGill University. She teaches courses in applied linguistics and ethnographic research. Her recent research examines the relationship between teachers' beliefs and assumptions about language and learning of minority language children and their teaching practices.

Kathy Mathers is English department chair at Washington Irving Junior High School in Colorado Springs, Colorado. She was a member of an